TROUBLESHOOTING FOR TRAINERS

Troubleshooting for Trainers

Getting it right when things go wrong

Lucy Seifert and Mary Stacey

Gower

Published by
Gower Publishing Limited
Gower House
Croft Road
Aldershot
Hampshire GU11 3HR
England

Gower
Old Post Road
Brookfield
Vermont 05036
USA

Lucy Seifert and Mary Stacey have asserted their right under the Copyright,
Designs and Patents Act 1988 to be identified as the authors of this work.

British Library Cataloguing in Publication Data
Seifert, Lucy
   Troubleshooting for trainers
   1. Employees – Training of – Evaluation 2. Employee training personnel
   I. Title II. Stacey, Mary
   658.3'12404

   ISBN 0 566 07914 3

Library of Congress Cataloging-in-Publication Data
Seifert, Lucy, 1948–
   Troubleshooting for trainers: getting it right when things go wrong / Lucy
   Seifert and Mary Stacey.
      p. cm.
   Includes index.
      ISBN 0–566–07914–3 (hardback)
   1. Employees–Training of.   2. Training.   I. Stacey, Mary, 1943–.   II. Title.
HF5549.5.T7S372   1998
658.3'124–dc21   98–16754
                                                                                  CIP

Phototypeset in 10/12 pt Palatino by Intype London Ltd. Printed in Great Britain
by Biddles Ltd, Guildford.

Contents

Preface

This book reveals some trainers' secrets. Other people usually don't spot these – or if they do, they are simply silent witnesses. It is about how we, the trainers, manage the people we meet, the participants, in a variety of contexts and situations. The stories are based mainly on trainers' experiences of dealing with 'trouble'.

When we started researching for this book we expected to find that trainers working in particular specialisms would have very different perceptions of training. However, we soon discovered that, although the content of a course might call for a particular style, there is much in common throughout the training field. Whether you are training, for example, in IT, sales, or personal development, you still have to deal with people's different natures, idiosyncrasies and attitudes to learning. You can assume nothing about people, and indeed, to do so can invite trouble.

The idea for *Troubleshooting for Trainers* arose when an IT trainer who had read Lucy Seifert's manual, *Training for Assertiveness*, commented, 'I like what you've done, but why don't you write something for all trainers'. Therefore, although our approach is influenced greatly by our own experience in assertiveness training, nevertheless this book is intended for *all* trainers.

Our approach to training is based on a number of fundamental principles. First, we believe intrinsically in equality between trainer and trainees. Secondly, we treat people as individuals, each of whom wants something different from training and has distinctive skills and experience to contribute, and we value this diversity. Thus training must take into account the identity, needs, ability and potential of each individual. Thirdly, equality of opportunity is an integral part of our philosophy. Opportunity must be available – or must be made available – to each individual on an equal basis, irrespective of gender, status, ethnic origin, colour, disability, sexual orientation, age, class, religion, creed, or political affiliation.

On practical issues, we see clear communication as the most vital element of training, and we try to avoid any jargon or format that may be exclusive or ambiguous. At the same time, we realize that participants' views may differ from our own; they may have different ways of doing things, or may simply disagree with what we say. The trainer may therefore have to confront the participant, and in doing so, we believe it is vital to concentrate on the content of the matter, and not to personalize the issue or attempt to put down the individual concerned.

As you read on, you will find that we can laugh now about some of the incidents we describe. Yet we can also remember what it felt like at the time to be upset or annoyed by the actions or comments of participants. What we sincerely hope is that we never allowed ourselves to be dismissive or arrogant in our response to such situations. It is always well worth remembering that, even though our objective is to impart new skills and knowledge, the trainees in turn have a great deal that they can teach us.

We don't of course have all the answers; as trainers we shall continue to learn throughout our careers. What we do have, though, is responsibility to the people we train – a responsibility to prepare ourselves for our task with the best methods and means, and a responsibility to keep an open mind, explore new ideas, and to suggest fresh solutions and new ways of doing things wherever possible.

Moreover, we have to create a safe and trusting learning environment, in which encouragement and enthusiasm allow people to learn from us and from each other. The immediate rewards for us as trainers lie in seeing the participants joining in and having fun in their training, bouncing ideas off each other and being creative, and also in watching both them and ourselves develop as a result of our efforts. In the end, providing we have fulfilled our part efficiently, the choice lies with them. They have to take the responsibility for learning.

Training can be a lonely and stressful job, especially if you work on your own. Sessions may go well, but afterwards you have to face the evaluations alone. In addition, your material has to be kept constantly fresh and stimulating, and you yourself must always remain positive and interested, even after a late night or a long, heavy week. One person in the group disrupts the session – you have to deal immediately and effectively with the situation. Certainly it's tough at times and, like actors, we need reassurance from both our audience and our peers.

Recognizing this need, we have set up a support group among our peers. As freelance trainers, we needed somewhere where we could share our successes, exchange ideas, and, above all, discuss our problems and aspects of the work that we found difficult to manage. This group has proved excellent for this purpose and has been most successful.

Thus even as experienced trainers, we continue to ask questions and seek advice, looking all the time for new ideas and exercises, fresh approaches, that will both revitalize our training sessions and facilitate our work. For we find that we frequently come face to face with new dilemmas, new complexities to deal with. No matter how many courses we have presented or groups we have tutored, the unexpected happens. Such moments can be inspiring and exciting, but on occasion they undermine and make you wonder, at least momentarily, why on earth you agreed to take this course.

So troubleshooting – the ability to resolve problems quickly and coolly – is, in our view, an integral part of all training. You too will have encountered tricky moments or challenges in your work, probably more often than not when you were working creatively or learning a new aspect of training. We believe it will be helpful, therefore, to look at the ways in which a number of trainers, working in different styles and in different environments, cope with, and indeed make the most of, such situations.

A terrible moment

The terrible moment usually happens unexpectedly. Everything seems to be going well. You have worked with the group for a day, and they are all being co-operative and working well together. Feeling confident, you start the second day by asking the participants how they are feeling and what they consider they gained from the previous day's work. And then comes the bombshell: 'Frankly, I thought yesterday was a complete waste of time. I very nearly didn't come today.'

When this happens, particularly if you are relatively inexperienced as a freelance trainer and perhaps working for a new client, the effect can be devastating. Your mouth goes dry, and you start to wonder how you are going to survive the moment, let alone get through the rest of the day. Was yesterday a waste of time? Would another trainer have approached it quite differently and done it so much better? Anxiety, worry and self-doubt begin to creep in.

With increasing experience you will learn how to handle this situation, despite its initial traumatic impact. After all, you have worked hard, and spent many hours preparing this course. You ask the participant to explain, please, why he or she feels this way, and you then check with the rest of the group what they think. Most often you will find that this is an isolated case, that this participant is the only member of the course who feels dissatisfied. Yet it is his or her voice that reverberates in your head, and you hardly hear all the others who say, 'I'm finding it very helpful. The course seems to be just what I wanted.'

A marvellous moment

The man rang and said: 'I want to thank you. I was so inspired by your course that I've resigned from my firm. There's another job I've been wanting to apply for for years, and now I'm going to have a go for it.'

You swallow hard. Here is a genuine compliment, a delighted participant, but his message still comes as rather a shock. Your remarks about risk-taking on the final day of the course certainly seem to have struck home. 'I do appreciate your call,' you reply. 'Will you please phone again and let me know how things go.'

Afterwards, you run through in your mind what you actually said on the course. Did you expect people to take your advice quite so literally? You begin to feel rather guilty, and more than a little worried. Did you actually advise him to give notice? What if he doesn't get that post and can't find another job quickly ... or for ages ... or at all? Will it be your fault if he's unemployed and terribly hard-up? Will he phone again and blame you for his predicament? Did he ... did you ... will he ...? And so you torture yourself.

Then you start to breathe deeply again. Putting your emotions to one side, you remind yourself that you acted in an entirely professional manner on the course. You imparted skills and ideas, and gave all the participants tools with which to make choices – what they do with those tools is their responsibility, not yours. Herein lies the difference: your role is to enable, the participants' role is to act.

Thus even apparent success may involve anxiety and stress, when reason and emotions vie with each other for the upper hand. In this instance, the participant was very pleased. No matter what may follow, he had found the courage to do what he had wanted to do for a long time. All you can do now is to wait for him to phone again.

At last the phone rings: 'You know that job I went after, well, I got it. And it was your remarks that gave me the inspiration. Can't thank you enough.' You smile down the phone. 'I really am very pleased for you. News like yours makes it all worthwhile.' Now that is a marvellous moment.

One predictable aspect of training is that both people and circumstances are unpredictable. Fortunately, most problems that occur are relatively minor, but they can and do occur on a daily basis. This book looks at you, the trainer, and at these challenges that you are likely at some stage to face.

If together we can explore both the pitfalls and pleasures of training, we can find ways to pre-empt some problems and better prepare ourselves to meet the rest.

Finally, in writing this book, we found that the bad moments in our training experience stood out, while the good moments were harder to recall. Isn't that so often the case? How easy it is to ignore or forget the voices that said, 'This has been the best course I've ever been on.'

Lucy Seifert
Mary Stacey

Lucy Seifert and Mary Stacey are pleased to offer guidance and training for groups or individuals. Based on the approach in this book, we tailor courses and individual work to meet your specific needs.
Visit our website at www.for-trainers.com
or e-mail us on lucy.seifert@for-trainers.com
mary.stacey@for-trainers.com

Acknowledgements

In the course of preparing and writing this text we have talked to many representatives from training organizations, trainers, both freelance and in-house, counsellors, managers, course participants, and many others. They have helped us with questionnaires, formal and informal interviews, presentation and format, anecdotes and experiences, and simply in general discussion that has sparked off new ideas and jogged old memories. Our sincere thanks to them all for their advice and help, and especially to the following:

- IT training consultant Saul Judah who first gave us the idea for this book.
- Diana Buirski, Jonathan Freilich, Breda Hill, Celia Levy and Teresa Rand at the City Literary Institute.
- John Anderson of GBS Training Ltd; Clare Branton of Resource IT; Margaret Burden, Innovations Manager of Community Service Volunteers; Suzi Dale of Training Today; Alison David; Paul De Ste Croix of Central London ITEC; Lesley Dee; David Fletcher; David Goodhart, Senior Social Worker at the North London Hospice; Gill Howe of Oxfordshire Social Services Training Section; Michael Jacobs, author and Director of Counselling and Psychotherapy Programme, University of Leicester; Margaret Lally; Denis Lloyd; Sarah Morland; Shirley Otto; Bob Richards; Josephine Seccombe; Sabina Seifert; Lisa Shortland; Ruth Sonntag of Grassroots Project; Mary Sturt of GBS Training Ltd; and Moira Walker, author, psychotherapist and trainer.
- Our own trainer support group of June Barnett, Sukey Field, Suzanne Greaves, Kareen Morgan, Chris Peters and Jennifer Roberts.
- Gower authors Sarah Cook, Geof Cos, Terry Gillen, Mary Griffiths, Di Kamp, Shona Mitchell, Teresa Williams and Terry Wilson.

- June Elks, who typed up our drafts and put them into a presentable whole with great efficiency and remarkable accuracy.
- Malcolm Forbes for the careful editing of the text.
- Malcolm Stern, who, as Gower's commissioning editor, has both encouraged and guided us through the project.
- All the course participants we have met over the years and who have taught us so much. Without them this book would not have been possible.

Finally, our thanks also to each other, for we have thoroughly enjoyed writing this book together.

LS
MS

Introduction

Who is this book for?

Troubleshooting for trainers is both for the new trainer and for the highly experienced. It is for the internal and external trainer, and for the person buying in or organizing the training. Even if, as a manager, you only arrange an occasional day's training with your staff, or simply facilitate one or two hourly sessions, you will find something here for you.

As well as drawing on our own extensive training experiences to write this book, we have asked trainers in diverse fields to tell us their tales, both tough and terrific. Whether you work in the public sector and utilities (e.g. social services, education, health, housing, gas, electricity); in voluntary organizations and charities, large and small; in counselling or complementary therapies; in commerce, from the small business to the large corporation – you will find here issues that affect you. Although the context and environment may be different, no matter where people work many of their training needs coincide. This includes a learning environment conducive to enhancing skills, knowledge and confidence.

The process

In this book we examine some of the problems you can face as a trainer and ways of overcoming those problems. Here you will find everyday as well as uncommon situations. We have deliberately included both more and less obvious troubles and tips.

They are based on actual experience revealed in our discussions and interviews with practising trainers.

You may look at these tales and think 'That sounds like me'. Indeed, by the time we reached the end of the book we couldn't always tell whose story it was. The tales are true, but the people and contexts have been changed for the sake of anonymity.

The metaphor

We have used the device of a metaphor, by likening the trainer to the performer and participants to an audience. While we do not view training as 'acting', we do identify elements in common such as 'first night nerves', 'stage fright', 'forgetting your lines' or 'being booed or applauded'. Nor do we view participants purely as an audience, since we regard interactive training as the most effective. However, the 'audience' response – whether they hang onto your every word or heckle you off the stage – will surely affect your performance or your self-esteem.

We look first at the performer (the trainer), and we start by describing what we see as training and the contrasting styles of delivery. We then see how trainers themselves can inadvertently ask for trouble, either when training alone or when co-training, and what they could do to avoid or deal with it. At the same time, we reassure those who are new to training that their anxieties and difficulties are not unusual.

After covering the practical aspects of your relationship with the person 'directing' or 'buying in' the training, we move on to the problems of staying fresh, particularly when you are an experienced trainer and have hundreds of training sessions behind you. The importance of practising what you preach is emphasized, and we set against this the strains of role modelling when you yourself are feeling either fragile or weary.

Recognizing first that you can become caught up in situations and face dilemmas because of conflicting agendas and demands made of you, we then face those first moments on stage when performer and audience meet, exploring the hotchpotch of troubles that the audience can present to the performer. There are participants too shy to speak and others too egotistical to stop, while some just treat training as a joke or would far prefer to be elsewhere. We look at ways of managing genuine reluctance as well as the games people play.

The group dynamic also has a profound effect on the training. In this context, we cite examples of trainers using all their diplomatic skills to restore and maintain a healthy balance in the group. Then there is the totally unexpected to deal with, which may be entertaining or downright difficult, is certainly always surprising, but is nevertheless all part of the training experience.

As a trainer your performance may be well rehearsed, but it is also impromptu, which allows you the flexibility to respond to a range of individuals and their needs. We analyse the issues posed by groups with different timing and pacing, and examine crises – matters both mechanical and personal, such as the video monitor breaking down, or the monstrous moment when you've prepared for five participants and fifty arrive.

The final chapter is all about endings. It covers the Oscars, the moment we've all been waiting for, yet fear. What will they think of me? How do you cope with difficult feedback? And at the end, how do you and they say all our goodbyes?

Troubles there may be in profusion, therefore, but if that were all there was to it, why would we do the job? Even some of the troubles are fun – albeit with hindsight. Thus the epilogue presents the magic moments of training, the laughs, the drive, and the inspiration.

The format

Each chapter contains a selection of problems that you could face before, during or after training. We describe the generic problem, then select specific troubles and ways of managing them. In some we present possible answers; others are illustrated by a case study showing how the trainer dealt with the difficulty.

Language

We call the people who come to training courses 'participants'. We know that they may also be referred to as delegates, trainees, course members or students, but we wanted to use a generic term and have chosen this one to emphasize that training is a participative activity. The term 'trainee' is used when we are making a clear distinction between the trainer and the participant – for example, the 'reluctant trainee'.

We use the term 'organization' to mean a business, company, local authority, voluntary organization or specific workplace. We have done this to ensure anonymity and also because we find that trainers' experience crosses organizational boundaries.

How to use this book

Dip in to the topics relevant to you, as and when you meet them. Alternatively, read from cover to cover so that you can incorporate tips into training and prevent some of the troubles from arising in the first place.

Our view is that there is no one way to deal with any problem, but rather a range of alternatives to draw from. Some may not be 'solved', but rather at best minimized or accommodated. Just as we encourage participants to choose their own solutions, so we leave it to you to find one, or several, or different combinations from the guidelines, depending on your personality, your training approach, and the group or individual that you are dealing with and their circumstances.

No book can possibly cover every eventuality or every way of dealing with the difficulties we have chosen to highlight. Knowing that others share our troubles is helpful in itself. A trouble shared is a trouble halved, though not necessarily solved. Reading this book will, we hope, reassure you that you are not alone and that other trainers have survived their troubles to train another day.

1 What is a trainer?

The aim of training is not to produce clones, but to alert participants to the issues they may have to encounter and offer skills and options in handling them.

The number of people calling themselves trainers is increasing. In this chapter we investigate how people see training, first giving our view of what training is and then examining the different ways that trainers perform. We draw attention to the number of people involved in training, and finish with the in-house trainer's view and the external trainer's view.

The trainer's role

The room goes silent.
  'What do you do?', someone asks.
  'I'm a trainer.'
  'But what do you *do*?'

You try to explain. If you say, I teach adults, that could be the end of the matter. But do you really see it like that? And what about course participants? Ask them about their experience of training and these will range from 'being lectured at' to 'forming into groups and exchanging ideas with colleagues', or from 'a complete waste of time' to 'it made me think and changed my way of working'.

  'I feel quite different as a trainer from being a lecturer,' explained a trainer. 'I still come with a theoretical base, but what I offer must be grounded in practice. You need to understand the jobs people are doing even if you haven't done exactly the same. It's helping people "look the right way." '

  You don't need to have all the answers. Your participants will produce their own answers if you allow them to bring something to the learning process too. You must be able to ask the right questions. There will be some skill-oriented courses, where there are right and wrong answers. And of course, it's a waste of time asking people to state the obvious when you know the answer already. But when asked 'What do you think I should do?', you may not want or be able to tell someone exactly. It depends on the circumstances and on them. You help them find and choose the options which will work for them.

In this book, we present guidelines for the trainer, suggesting different ways of working. Some will suit you, others will not, but the choice is yours. This is how we see training. It is not lecturing *at* people, although you certainly give information. A good trainer does not dominate, yet exercises authority within the group. You may challenge people's practice, but you must preserve their self-esteem. You share your knowledge and skills, but you don't deskill. You show people how to do things, but *they* have to do something too.

The focus is on the participants' learning; the trainer, although crucial in this process, takes a secondary role at times. An organization, describing its training as vocational and measurable, emphasizes the importance of empowering through participation, and the delicate balance held by the trainer. As one of their staff explained:

> Some trainers, regarding themselves as 'naturals', skip the preparation and work too intuitively. The entertainer type may be dynamic and the audience have a good time, but they don't learn and develop. They are passive listeners. Passive reception disempowers the audience whereas effective training empowers.

Training styles

Researching this book, we met successful trainers with many different styles on a continuum from extremely directive to 'laissez-faire'. As you train your style may vary. Indeed, within one day you may find yourself in each of the following roles:

- enabler;
- challenger;
- chairperson;
- lecturer;
- referee;
- adviser; and
- objective outsider.

Sometimes you tend towards a directive approach where you set out what you want people to do, or a co-ordinating one where you bring the participants' ideas and knowledge together in a less overt way.

Most trainers are directive at times, but how they define this style depends on how they perceive the act of training. One trainer described his way of directing: 'I tell people: this is what I believe in. This is how I think it works. Now let's discuss it and see what you think.' He brings his own skills and experience to the training but allows the participants to add theirs. The learning takes place through the discussions and exercises, but people also need concrete facts and figures and a sense of direction.

Some trainers described themselves as 'low-key' in their approach. This could sound as if they did very little. However, we see this style as leading a group, rather like a shepherd, knowing where you want to go with them but not necessarily leading from the front all the time, moving with the group but bringing them back on track to reach the final goal. Low-key does not mean unprepared or weak. The following story which a trainer recounted illustrates this. A person setting up a training session had heard that the trainer had a good reputation but was 'quiet'. Worried that the trainer might not be able to manage a potentially difficult group, she phoned to discuss the situation. The trainer quoted an evaluation sheet that someone had written the week before: 'I liked the trainer; she was low-key but very powerful.' Others adopting this style have been described as 'gentle but challenging'.

We asked trainers if they felt they were charismatic in their style. Some definitely saw themselves as the central character and their role as that of inspirational leader. Others were doubtful until we defined charisma as a way of inspiring enthusiasm, not just as a personal attribute. 'I think I must be', said one, 'because people take away my ideas and want to do what I say.'

You may work with very small groups or a hall full of people, with senior managers or domestic staff. Yet wherever you train, whether you train in personal development or technical skills, and whatever your style, we believe that good trainers have much in common. They bring their own personalities into the room but share common principles about the function of training.

Trainers work best when they take into account the expressed but varied needs of individuals or organizations, offering a clear framework of content which is relevant to people's different learning skills and styles. The successful trainer is well organized, and has clear scripts and well-defined aims and objectives which enable individuals and groups to bring to the surface abilities and skills that they may not have recognized in themselves.

You come across people who are stuck, demotivated or demoralized.

Your job is to show them how to peel off the layers of their difficulty, helping them to identify one or two things they can do to move forward. There are others who are successful, enthusiastic, open and ready to analyse what they are doing. In this case, you have the challenge and excitement of putting your skills and experience together with theirs so that they can develop further.

Training frameworks have to be flexible. You must be ready for the unexpected and ready to pick up the opportunities for learning which arise. Despite this flexibility, however, people need to know why they are there, and to be able to follow you with conviction, knowing what they can achieve from the training. You may travel a long way during your time together, but you have to follow a clear route. One trainer summed it up as follows:

> I present and reinforce the clarity by:
> - giving out an outline with the objectives;
> - doing;
> - summarising and reviewing the content and learning.

Involving others is risky – it's also the exciting part of training. Asked what they enjoyed most, experienced trainers said it was being the catalyst for learning and seeing people moving on. You have to have faith that people learn for themselves; you can't do that part for them.

In-house and external trainers

The stories in this book come from both in-house and external trainers. Although their relationship with an organization is different, we have found that their experience of face-to-face training is often very similar. Let us consider, therefore, what trainers see as the advantages and disadvantages of being inside or outside an organisation. The issues mentioned are explored later in the book.

The in-house trainer's view

> I find there are many advantages to being an in-house trainer. But it depends where you are employed. If training is regarded as an easy option then people seem to work on Shaw's maxim, 'He who can, does. He who cannot, teaches.' Employees who are in danger of being made redundant or have failed in another part of the organization are put into

the training department. Sometimes these appointments work out, but it's not good for us, for them or for the status of training.

Although it is essential as an in-house trainer to earn your own personal status through experience and reputation, the training department also needs status or no one takes it seriously.

You are an easy target for criticism. You can be regarded as part of the bureaucracy, yet because you are in a non-managerial role, people feel that they can direct their anger at you. Like external trainers, you must develop a sound reputation. You can do this by being fair and understanding, and by offering practical and relevant training. Once people recognize and value your experience, then there are lots of advantages.

Understanding the working context well means that you establish a way of working operationally and consultatively. This may take time as you get to know and work with the managers, and find out where the strengths and weaknesses in the organization are. Once you have established your position, though, the reward lies in devising long-term programmes with the managers, receiving their backing, and involving them in the follow-up and evaluation. You can see changes taking place, and you are not just doing one-off programmes which the participants may enjoy but no one else really takes much notice of.

By meeting you regularly over the years, participants come to know and like you and to feel comfortable with you. Nevertheless, you have to keep some distance and avoid becoming the person they bring their troubles to or try to draw into a situation which is not your concern. You must make it very clear that you cannot work miracles or immediately resolve problems for people. On the other hand, you can become the conduit, feeding ideas back and forth, and liaising between different view points. You learn from the participants what is working, and what is not. Thus you can play a part in challenging practice both inside and outside the training room, and you can influence policies through your 'objective' position. Indeed, as an in-house trainer, you can wield substantial influence.

It is true that the external trainer can say exactly what he or she thinks, while as an in-house trainer you have to choose your words carefully and often compromise. This can be helpful, however, insofar as you learn to be realistic and to create ways of helping people forward without promising them what you know they will never attain.

Becoming known within the organization and developing good relationships with the other employees and managers is an important part of the job. There may be a dilemma when you recognize bad practice. Participants must be able to trust you, but you must also be alert to bad practice which may be harmful or dishonest. That is why your position as trainer needs to be quite clear. Everyone must know where the confidentiality begins and ends, and this is especially important if you work part-time in another role within the organization.

You must offer training which relates to what people are doing, and you require knowledge and experience of their work to do this. So even if you have never done their job, you must find out about it. An external trainer might get away with a bad day's training – they're only in for one day – but an in-house trainer has to come in the next day, and the next.

The external trainer's view

> I left the business because I was fed up with the politics. There's a myth that you make a fortune as a trainer and that it's easy money. It depends where you work. I don't see it like that. You have to work hard to succeed as an independent trainer. I think I work harder than I ever did before. But I love being my own boss and the variety of the work. You never know what will come next.

Like the in-house trainer, you have to earn your reputation. Unlike them, you are judged on every job. This can be a strain, but it also keeps you alert and up to date. If you become careless and slapdash, you will not be invited back. Trainers working alone suggest it takes about three years to become fully established. For most, there are the anxious moments when you wonder where the next job is coming from, and you become familiar with the pattern of 'feast or famine' in your work.

Working in a training organization means you have administrative back-up and also colleagues to discuss and develop ideas with. On your own, you usually start out doing everything, and that can be lonely. Gradually though, you build a network of trusted colleagues among other trainers and people for whom you work. Moreover, you choose your close working colleagues, unlike having to be friendly with whoever else is in an organization, which is the in-house trainer's lot.

It can be both an advantage and a disadvantage not belonging anywhere. You are frequently going into something new, and you must learn the background quickly, researching the organization and finding out their training needs, the key issues at stake, and current practice. You can be badly caught out by not knowing all the detailed background to your client and the commission. Also, people may see you as a convenient receptacle for all their moans and complaints. If you don't know the background you can end up colluding with whoever is in front of you.

Of course, you do build up special relationships with organizations and the people in them, and you can come to feel very much part of the place. One difficulty in this, however, is that people forget that you work elsewhere, and if they do remember, they are not terribly interested. As far as they are concerned, you're one of them when you're working for them. When they ring up to speak to you and you are absorbed in another piece of work, they assume that their job is uppermost in your mind – and indeed it has to be while they are talking.

The main advantage of not belonging to the organization is being able to see clearly what is going on and not being emotionally involved in the situation. This is an obvious benefit for the participants and you can use your objectivity to great effect. You can speak plainly and suggest radical ways of doing things, although you have to be realistic. Having no direct involvement and not being part of the establishment means you can take an unbiased look at the problem and help people sort out the issues. Trainers talk of the way that they can see and assess situations more clearly from their position than they could when they themselves were part of a group or organization, and how much easier it is to find solutions. You have to remember that as a trainer you have a bird's eye view: that is, you are seeing the whole, rather than just a part. At the same time, you have to judge the situation from the participants' point of view as well, and you must be careful not to take sides.

Being able to leave everything behind can also be a blessing. You walk out at the end of the day and your job is finished. The downside to that is lack of involvement in long-term planning and follow-up on particular issues; nor do you see the results of the training. Furthermore, if you work alone, you can find that there is no one to talk things through with at the end of the training session. On the other hand, if you feel you are not the right person for the job or you don't want to work with an organization, you can say 'no' to work.

External trainers, like the internal trainer, learn a great deal while doing the job. In addition, they can control their own schedule and, while they have to earn a living, they can decide to take time to develop other interests and skills. Both internal and external trainers agree that you need energy and enthusiasm to be a trainer, and you must be ready for any eventuality. Working together can offer a superb combination. Internal and external trainers offer different viewpoints and experiences, combining objectivity with a close understanding of what is going on.

Summary

You may be a training manager, training administrator, training consultant, a direct trainer, or a combination of these. Boundaries between these roles blur and your role will vary depending on where you work. You are likely to be in, or perceived to be in, several training roles, and even if you are not, you will have to relate to and negotiate with others in those roles. The clearer the lines of communication between those involved, the better.

You may be a training manager whose responsibility is to:

- understand what is happening in the organization and who is involved;
- assess the staff and the organization's needs;
- make decisions with managers about appropriate training;
- budget realistically;
- motivate staff through training;
- consult with trainers and agree clear objectives and content;
- debrief the trainers;
- initiate new training; and
- evaluate training and continue or modify it accordingly.

External trainers particularly need to know how courses are administrated. The responsibilities of a training administrator include:

- day-to-day organization and paperwork;
- arranging venues, participant lists, resources, equipment, refreshments, and so forth;
- carrying out administration for the trainer (e.g. sending out pro-grammes, organizing handouts); and
- monitoring and recording attendance, the training carried out and evaluations.

There is often a thin line between the role of direct trainer and consultant. Many trainers act as both, carrying out the training programme and con-sulting before and after the training. In-house trainers are also often in this position, working operationally and consultatively within the organisation. A training consultant:

- gives advice on policy and practice;
- carries out training needs analysis; and
- works closely with managers, advising on management, staff and project development.

This book deals with the direct trainer, both in-house and external, whose work involves:

- training groups face to face
- running training sessions on specific, designated topics – often skills based, such as IT or meeting skills;

- devising and tailoring training to perceived needs; and
- preparing and planning the training materials and/or delivering pre-packaged training.

2 Asking for trouble

It's the best job in the world if you like doing it; it's the worst if you don't.

As this book is about troubleshooting, we have to acknowledge that the trainer too can be the troublemaker. Therefore, in the first part of this chapter, we find out how easy it is to ask for trouble, and how important it is to put yourself into the participants' shoes and feel what it is like to be on the receiving end. In the second part, we examine how you can often avoid trouble by: finding out about the participants; careful preparation; understanding your role as the trainer; and developing working partnerships with co-trainers.

Talking about trouble

Trainers don't usually go out of their way to 'ask for trouble', but most of us have done so inadvertently at some time or other. Too late you realize that someone is offended or upset by something you have said unthinkingly, or you misjudge the mood, touch on people's raw spots, even lose your temper.

Many of you are no doubt your own severest critic, but it is not always easy for trainers to admit their mistakes to their peers, especially if you are working in a competitive environment. We asked a group of trainers if and when they had asked for trouble. They were in no doubt that they had done so at times, but agreed that it could be difficult to talk about, either because they felt foolish or had handled a situation badly.

Most trainers experience feelings of both power and vulnerability. You have a group of people doing what you suggest, but at the same time you know that you are constantly being judged. Is that what makes some

15

trainers defensive? What is the pressure that makes you feel you can't admit you made a mistake?

We believe that the best trainers feel a degree of discomfort about what they do. It is not a question of denigrating yourself but you do need continually to be aware of the impact you are having and to check on the quality of the learning process and your input. It is easy to grow stale or to take things for granted. When you have had a successful time with a group, you can't rest on your laurels for long because next time will bring different people, different issues. In most courses, you are asking people to change, but you need to change also. You are asking people to be open, so you try to create an environment in which they can feel safe. Yet trainers need safe places too – places where you can find colleagues with whom it's possible to be open, admit mistakes, receive support, and discuss and develop ideas.

Troubled times

You have a bad day when your exercises – usually energizing and thought provoking – go down like a lead balloon. Sometimes you can rescue the situation, and that is what this book concentrates on. At other times you are so tired that you become impatient or find yourself ill-prepared and led off track. We all have moments when we wish we had done things differently or feel that we didn't do as well as we could.

Read through the following list from other trainers. Do you recognize any of these occasions when you asked for trouble? Be honest with yourself, and realize that it happens to others too. You:

- involve yourself in an argument which is not pertinent to the training;
- find yourself in the middle of a story which you suddenly realize isn't relevant, or, worse still, you forget the punch line;
- bluff your way through something or pretend you know what the latest jargon means;
- let a group wander off the point;
- give an inappropriate response by your body language;
- push someone too hard to do something they don't want to do;
- concentrate on an individual to the exclusion of others;
- flirt with someone in the group;
- go on too long with an exercise or with your own input;
- allow yourself to be sidetracked by a participant;
- get bored and lose concentration;
- give double messages (e.g. asking unassertively for people to do things assertively);

- say, 'I want you to do this', when in fact you haven't thought through the instruction or are scared of the results;
- make a poor judgement of a participant (e.g. you're duped by the initial impression, or you don't allow enough time for feedback, with the result that the group's feelings are stifled or grow out of proportion);
- miss the main point;
- tell people, 'We haven't time to do this', so that they feel they are being short changed, or they become anxious;
- give them an unrealistic programme that you cannot possibly complete.
- rush through the work and misjudge the time;
- come down hard on someone you think can take it because he or she appears strong and confident;
- go on after the finishing time without letting people know why you are doing this;
- don't check on people's experience and their roles at work;
- forget some important information;
- make assumptions that people will respond in a certain way because they work in a particular area (e.g. banking, selling, teaching, social work);
- rush someone who doesn't understand and needs more time;
- cut corners;
- think, 'This will be a walkover. It worked well when I did it last time, so I don't need to prepare anything this time.'
- miss the important parts from participants' feedback;
- allow others to put down someone in the group;
- don't facilitate the feedback from participants to each other, so that it becomes negative or out of order;
- misjudge the impact of role play.

On the receiving end

You learn a great deal about training if you step into the role of participant and attend training sessions yourself. You observe the trainer – group interrelationship. You realize what it feels like to be on the receiving end of unclear instructions or badly thought out objectives. You might experience what happens when a trainer lacks empathy for her or his group. Many trainers learn much about the techniques of training through their own bad experiences as trainees, as the following trainers' tales illustrate.

Lost trust

> I was attending a session on equal opportunities. When the trainer said, 'Things aren't always black and white', I said I didn't like the use of that phrase. I said it politely. But she turned on me: 'That's your problem,' she said. She lost me from that moment.

Inappropriate activities

> I go on courses regularly because it helps me to develop my own skills. I'm interested in the way that trainers set the scene and I gain many ideas from them. But on this occasion, I couldn't believe what I was hearing. The trainers used an icebreaker, asking lots of questions to help people to mix. We had to move places depending whether the answer was 'Yes' or 'No', and talk to the people we met. It was going all right and we were mixing together when out of the blue, they said, 'Anyone move who hasn't had sex in the last six months'. Did they think it was funny? I didn't, especially as I had recently broken up with a partner. I froze. That was the end as far as I was concerned.

False assumptions

> I work with groups of women and often people become very close. But what I can't bear is a forced intimacy. I was on a training for trainers course – we'd been together for about two days. The trainer read out a story all about fuzzies. I don't know what relevance it had to the course, but suddenly she was saying, 'Now before you go home, we'll all give each other a fuzzy' – she meant a hug. Well, I'm all for hugging my friends, but not under instruction. I could see that one or two other participants felt the same as me, but not conforming to the group somehow seemed standoffish. Anyway, I didn't join in, and I went home feeling uncomfortable and extremely annoyed.

These participants, although trainers themselves, found it difficult to challenge or to express how they felt. Their experiences emphasize the importance of creating an openness between the trainer and trainees from beginning to end of each course.

Knowing who's there

As the tales above illustrate, making assumptions about how people will react and behave asks for trouble. You can certainly do some research beforehand about the group, and even if you cannot find out much, you are at least able to create an environment in which people can let you know about themselves and how they see things.

Taking into account different learning preferences is essential. Some participants will have attended a number of training courses. They will know what is expected of them, may even have done your exercises before, and will understand what you mean by such terms as 'feedback', 'brainstorm', and 'role play'. Also they will be prepared to play an active part. Others may be new to training or to your style or may have had bad experiences of being lectured at or of experiential learning. To this group you will have to explain how you work and what you expect from them.

Recognizing cultural differences and giving people opportunities to contribute their experiences, which may well differ from your own, will help everyone to learn. Since in some cultures questioning the teacher is seen as impolite, trainers can make it clear that they want participants to join in and ask for information. One trainer in doing this sensitively changed her usual 'Are there any questions?' to 'What questions do you have on the material?' Another trainer told us how she learnt the hard way, assuming that people would not mind holding hands in an exercise, only to find that it was culturally unacceptable to some of her participants.

If you always make sure at the start that there is access for people with disabilities, and that everyone can hear you, see the overheads, and move easily into small groups, then these checks become an integral part of the training and not something tacked on or 'special.' And taking note of age and gender differences between you and within the group, makes you aware of any dynamics within the relationships.

You may not remember the names of everyone, but if you make no assumptions to start with and are open to everyone, you are likely to know a great deal about the participants by the end. 'I couldn't do it if I didn't find people interesting,' said one trainer. 'I like to know who's actually there behind the face.'

Knowing where you're going

'I see no point in being here', say some participants. This objection is one which many trainers have experienced during their careers. Therefore, as the trainer, you must know the purpose for which you are there and, in conjunction, the reasons why training needs were identified in the first place, so that you are quite clear in your own mind where you are taking the participants (the objectives or learning outcomes). If the organization isn't clear and neither are you, you can hardly expect the participants to know what they are doing there. Lack of clarity and direction is a recipe for dissatisfied customers.

Some organizations ensure that participants are fully briefed about courses in advance, while others give the participants little prior notice, and provide only the title of the course without offering details of content, aims and objectives, learning methods, or background information on the trainer. If this latter situation is compounded by you, the trainer, failing to provide a clear route at the outset of the training, difficulties may arise, because participants cannot understand why they are there in the first place, are confused about what you intend to do, and are unclear what they'll gain from the training.

Hence you can do much to make life easier for yourself and win over your participants before, at the start of and during the training by preparing both for yourself and for them. You can do this by the following means:

- Consulting with the organization about how the training need has arisen and what their objectives are.
- Planning and agreeing a programme.
- Informing participants about the programme, objectives and method of delivery.
- Consulting initially with the participants about *their* needs as distinct from the needs of the organization, in the event, of course, of there being any points of divergence, or differences in requirements.
- Indicating to the participants how you will incorporate their needs when they do differ from the organization's.
- Where it is not possible to meet all the varying, even conflicting, needs, clearly explaining that they are outside your remit but offering to pass on participants' further requirements to the appropriate person or to point them in the direction of further training.

Misinformed and uninformed

One trainer describes how:

> The participants arrived with differing levels of knowledge and expectation. One had been told only that morning to attend; another had chosen the course from a one-paragraph blurb in the training prospectus; another had discussed it with her manager at her appraisal; all but one had been given the title only, and one person told me it sounded like 'the rubbish we did last year'.

Advance notice

One way of ensuring that everyone starts with the same information is for you to provide it. You can send everyone a letter introducing yourself (if you're external), reminding them of the title, venue and timing, and saying that you are looking forward to working with them. You might want to add they are welcome to call you if they have any queries prior to the course. This approach helps create a link between yourself and participants before you meet, and also demonstrates that you are accessible. Moreover, it will give the more anxious participants an opportunity to 'meet' you by letter and to phone and allay some anxieties beforehand.

Accompanying this letter, send the course outline showing:

- title and sub-title;
- your aims;
- content;
- objectives/learning outcomes;
- your methods of training; and
- reading or other preparation they may wish to do.

What will I gain from the course?

You can diffuse much resentment or indifference expressed by participants towards training by clearly indicating what you are intending to cover, and importantly, what they will be able to achieve as a result. If people can see that there is a benefit for them in being able to do something either differently or for the first time as a result of working with you, you are well on your way, to winning them over.

To this end, objectives or learning outcomes are best described using action verbs to describe something observable. The following examples are drawn from different types of training:

By the end of the course participants will be able to:

- prioritize their work;
- organize a press conference;
- write minutes of a management council meeting;
- prepare a budget;
- mediate in a conflict between two individuals;
- chair a meeting effectively;
- develop a full, featured programme using C++.

By going through your objectives again at the start of a session, checking for understanding and additional requests, you demonstrate that you are keen for participants to be actively consulted and involved in the programme, even though it was initially designed and agreed between you and the training purchaser.

Off the shelf

However, you may be delivering the same course each time. You might be asked by an organization to give all their staff the same training. Or you may work for a training organization that offers pre-designed courses for staff attending from a range of companies and organizations. Your remit is to deliver off-the-shelf courses.

Clarify what you will cover, what the participants will be able to do as a result of your course, and how they will reach those goals. If you do leave room for an element of flexibility within off-the-shelf training, say so. Participants need to know whether there is time for questions and how client responsive, or not, they can expect the training to be.

You can put participants at their ease, or at least give them the right expectations if you inform them clearly of your approach and also:

- whether you use an interactive or lecture style;
- if there will be opportunities for questions;
- if they will be expected to do practical work;
- if the course is mainly hands-on; and
- whether each area of information will be consolidated by undertaking exercises using specific commercial examples relevant to their work.

Off-the-shelf training has its benefits and limitations, but if you allow participants to come to the session with expectations that differ from the reality of what you expect to give, you could be asking for trouble.

Unmet expectations

Participants having realistic expectations of a course is central to the success of training. Therefore, if there is a lack of clarity about content, objectives and methodology, or if you offer unrealistic expectations either as a carrot to encourage attendance or because you misjudge how much you and/or they can cover, or if the course is either too or insufficiently intensive or extensive, participants may well come away feeling inadequate or short-changed.

We discussed with participants their feelings about unmet expectations and how it affected their attitudes towards a specific training session and training in general. One disgruntled IT trainee told us:

I might as well have stayed at home and read the book. The trainer simply took us through the manual. I could've done that by myself. I wanted more than I could give myself, like some solid, real life examples. I needed to be able to test, under supervision, if I could use the software to deal with an extensive problem. By the end of the course I thought I'd be able to do that, because I'd learned the concepts and how to use the software during set exercises. What I hadn't appreciated at the time was that these were small, unrelated examples. When I got back to the office and was faced with a larger industrial problem, I couldn't do it. So I was none the wiser, and I had no one to ask.

The participant suggested that the trainer could have:

● described the course as 'following a manual'; and
● clarified the point that participants would have a grasp of theory and would have practised examples in applications, but that in order to be able to approach a problem holistically they would need to attend further training.

Alternatively, the trainer could have:

● researched the company;
● devised situations for use in practical application during the course so that participants could use them in their day-to-day work; and
● stated this in the course description.

   Participants stressed the importance of having accurate and precise information in advance of a course about what was offered, and what they would realistically learn and be able to do as a result of their learning. They could then make informed choices about what to attend. They would also feel more positive about the training they chose.

The lazy trainer

Other trainees complain about a complete lack of trainer input:

She just put us into groups to discuss questions, but she didn't do anything with this. She didn't look at the way we'd worked together, and she didn't sum up. She just set more questions. We could have done all this without her. She'd obviously done no preparation beforehand. That's a lazy trainer.

Knowing what to do

When the curtain rises, you can stick to your script or perform impromptu, but whatever your approach you must reach your dénouement before the curtain falls. How long you have to reach these objectives depends on the format. Are you working one-off with a group you don't know, or developing a relationship over several weeks or months? Your audience may have years of poor educational experience to undo, in which case you have to create a culture whereby people can unlearn and learn, where they can co-operate and blossom. You want your audience to have confidence in you and in what you are doing. Therefore, you have to gain and hold their attention, help them gel, then turn their attention back on themselves.

Here we look at being in the mood, displaying your confidence, creating the right atmosphere for the style, and developing the authority to draw the best from your audience and achieve the most for them.

Putting on the mood

An off-day or a day off?

I arrived late and disorganized. I couldn't get myself together. I just wasn't in the mood. I longed all day for the course to end. The participants were not exactly oblivious to my poor performance. My discomfort affected them. They looked agitated and I couldn't engage them. I wanted to crawl into a hole.

GUIDELINES

- If you decide that the show must go on, be a true professional. Take off your personal 'I'm not in the mood' hat and don your trainer's cap for the hours you are on stage.
- You can be yourself again as soon as you come off stage, though a riveting day's training may in itself change your mood, depending on what caused the problem in the first place.
- Be a positive role model to your group, or they won't be convinced. They will think you're a fake.
- Practise what you preach. The audience learn from observing and seeing that what you ask of them is achievable.
- The model you present, the atmosphere you create, depends much on how you come across as a person, confident, at ease with yourself and with others.
- Show authority without being authoritarian.
- Be high on assertion, low on aggression or passivity.

Displaying your confidence

One trainer felt she was a natural born actress and this helped her keep going however she felt. It was also useful in actively demonstrating a point.

Natural born actors

> Even when you're not in the mood, you'd rather be out walking the dog or sunbathing, you have to go out there and perform – and do it well! I think it's no coincidence that I used to act and sing. I feel my adrenalin flow when I'm centrestage. I gain pleasure from knowing my audience are with me. I forget everything else that's going on in my life.

Not all trainers have a natural confidence but develop their own style and ways of coping.

Cold feet

> I came into training by accident. I would never have chosen it. No matter how many sessions I do, I'm not that confident about being 'on stage'. To counter it, I prepare to perfection, and remind myself of the wealth of experience I've gained. It helps me keep calmer and relax into the session. By keeping in touch with my inner confidence, I can give the group confidence too.

GUIDELINES

- Show enthusiasm and enjoyment in what you do.
- Display confidence but not arrogance as a performer.
- If you show a gentle, unobtrusive confidence, your participants can develop a calm unspoken confidence in themselves, in each other and in you.
- Be empathetic towards your audience.
- Never put them down, but encourage them to work with you and each other to develop their skills.
- Keep monitoring your own performance.
- If you feel bored or uninterested, it's time to take stock, take a break, stop or do it differently. You owe that to yourself and to others. How boring is a bored trainer!

Creating the atmosphere

In each other we trust – or do we?

> Just for a change I decided to do some personal development for myself. I love occasionally, as a trainer, to attend courses run by other trainers at work. I went along open-minded, excited yet relaxed about being in the audience for a day. The experience stands out in my mind. Without any overture, the trainer went straight into the performance. I felt quite anxious. 'Aren't we going to agree confidentiality,' I asked. 'I took that for granted,' he replied. After that I could never concentrate properly on the course. I made superficial contributions, feeling anxious about digging too deeply, and came away with raised anxiety.

GUIDELINES

- Remember that you are not a performer in splendid isolation. You depend on your audience for success in attaining objectives.
- To fully engage participants and enable change, they need a safe climate in which they can feel free to ask questions, discuss issues, or say 'I don't understand'.
- Participants need to feel that the group, and you, are with them and for them.
- It is helpful as a trainer to experience being a participant from time to time in order not to lose touch with your audiences. You are reminded what is needed to feel safe, absorbed and to develop as a result of training. In addition, you learn from other trainers what not to do, and also gain positive tips and ideas.

Finding your style

The knowledge

> I'd been asked to take a group who were in the throes of change. It was clear from the start, though I'd not known in advance, how hostile they were to change. Based on my brief from management, I'd thoroughly researched for my part. 'All research shows . . .', I launched in, supporting my thesis with all manner of facts and figures. This was the last thing they wanted to hear. As the heckling began, I realized what it was like to be a politician. It was a stark lesson, but a useful one. I learned not to tell, but to train.

GUIDELINES

- Recognize that training may involve telling – but not imposing.
- Use telling only as a part. Above all, let people find their knowledge from within.
- Never impose your will, your view, or someone else's, on the group – you'll lose them.
- If you supply facts and figures, ask them their views, or what the learning is.

Using your authority wisely

You are invested with an authority which at one level can be stimulating and constructive, but which also brings with it enormous responsibility to use it properly and positively for others. At times you have to be tough – challenge, disagree with what's being said – but this you have to do while still respecting the group and mindful of your position in it. Humour helps tremendously to lighten the atmosphere, but not when it puts down others. Challenge provokes thoughts and action, but only when there is respect for the other person and the opportunity for discussion. Your own experience can be extremely helpful to others – so long as it is relevant.

Co-training

Co-training at its best has advantages for participants and trainers. The group benefits from two types of knowledge, experience and style, and can be energized by the change in personality and pacing when trainers are quite different. Trainers can support each other when difficulties arise, put their heads together to solve problems and share the enjoyment of successful training. However, if you're not a good role model during co-training, there is then twice the chance that it will go wrong.

Most problems cited by trainers with experience of co-training centred on lack of clarity about their roles. Sometimes one party did not openly either accept or reject the role assigned to them, thus leaving unclear boundaries between the two trainers, who perceived their roles differently from each other. For example, if one person is lead trainer and the other assisting, this can work well provided both parties agree their roles clearly in advance. Where clear agreements were not made in advance, but different roles emerged anyway, resentments built up. Here we tell some of the awkward experiences described by co-trainers, and suggest how to prevent them or manage them if they do arise.

Leading and learning to co-train

The first three stories illustrate the importance of understanding how you relate to each other, particularly when the experienced and less experienced work together. Learning to stand back and let someone do things differently from you is hard if you have been training successfully for years. Conversely, 'performing' in front of someone you admire, or feel may judge you, is inhibiting for the inexperienced.

Standing in his shadow

I once made the mistake of working with someone for whom I had immense respect, but in whose shadow I lost some of my respect for myself. He had formerly been my manager, had authority over me and considerably more experience. Though that hierarchy no longer existed between us, I couldn't see him any other way. When it came to co-training, I took a back seat, which was no fault of his. Sadly, it affected my self-esteem as a trainer for some time to come. I simply had not been ready at that stage to co-train with a highly experienced, confident and competent co-trainer.

Standing in my shadow

I had a gut feeling we wouldn't work well together. She had little experience, and I wanted an equal relationship. But she was so keen, I gave in. From that moment on her enthusiasm went and I made all the running. I initiated our planning, suggested the programme, led the group. She became barely more than an observer. I realized too late that that had been her intention, to observe. She'd said one thing, and done another, just to get her way. I'd allowed myself to be seduced by her reassurance of hard work in a supporting role, whereas I should have trusted my gut.

Letting go

'You don't have to protect me,' she said. 'I can do this.' I was quite shocked and rather hurt. I had believed I was supporting her. We'd discussed at length beforehand how we would present and who would do what. But I realized that as the experienced trainer in this partnership, I was jumping in, being helpful as I thought, but actually being very controlling. I wanted the training to be up to standard and I felt nervous seeing someone presenting for the first time. But she was quite right: she needed the freedom to develop her own style, to learn through doing it her way.

I learnt then that there are times when you take a back seat as the co-trainer, that the leadership of the session passes from one to the other. Of course you help each other out at times, but you must also trust each other and allow your different styles to emerge.

GUIDELINES

- Wait until you feel you have sufficient experience, confidence and competence before co-training with someone previously your senior.
- Discuss the previous status in relation to each other and how that hierarchy affects your feelings about working together now.
- Make an agreement between you, including how to role model and how to share responsibility.
- Agree who will open, who will close.
- Allocate the activities and agree how and when you can each chip in.
- Give equal input, within reason.
- Defer to each other appropriately during the course, illustrating respect for each other, and demonstrating it in front of the group.
- Never show each other up in front of your audience or display competition between you, even when one does know more than the other.
- If you feel you want to take a backseat during your first experience of co-training with someone, say so, setting out that your objectives are to contribute, to support and to learn; schedule your roles accordingly.
- Decide how you will clarify your roles to the group.
- In debriefing together, clarify continually how you see your roles and when you are ready to genuinely co-train, with as much equality of input and responsibility as is realistic.
- Talk about your own ways of doing things and how you may feel seeing someone deliver differently from you.
- Discuss who leads the session and when and what the role is for the other. Take it in turns to lead on different days or for different activities.
- As you work together, develop an understanding of when you want your co-trainer to contribute and when to take a back seat.

Developing partnerships

Trainers working in a trusting partnership often intuitively dovetail their changing roles during the training. The one takes a 'mental' break while observing the group, and the other takes the lead. At other times they become a double act, bouncing ideas off each other. 'I'll do it my way' and 'In the lurch' illustrate the difficulty when someone does not understand the responsibilities of the partnership, and how important it is to discuss how you will do it as well as what you will do.

I'll do it my way

> I was co-training a team-building course with a colleague. I hardly knew him, but, aware of his background in training, assumed that it would be an exciting joint venture. We planned and timed our agenda and content, and parcelled them out between us, clear about our individual roles and responsibilities. Or so I thought.
>
> Came the day of the training, and all the planning proved to have been worthless. My co-trainer completely ignored our script, taking the star role in a one-man show. I was the extra, the hired hand. My wealth of experience was kept locked away throughout the performance. I felt devalued, depressed and very angry.

The stooge

When you've trained with someone for a long time, you can become type-cast in a role that you may not like, and you can do this to yourself.

> I worked with a charismatic trainer. Groups found her riveting: she had lots of anecdotes, got all the laughs, was quick with repartee and never at a loss for words. Increasingly I assumed the role of 'fallguy', and that's where I stayed. It was an easy role to enter, but hard to escape from.
>
> One day I thought 'I'm not doing this any more. I need to train alone. I have charisma too.' But I knew that if I returned to the partnership, I'd revert to playing second fiddle.

This trainer woke up to the fact that she was good and therefore needed to move on. Her story illustrates how you can be held back by someone else, and how you take on different roles and styles depending on who you're with or whether you're training alone.

GUIDELINES

- Make no assumptions about each other.
- Complement and draw the best from each other's skills and qualities, for the benefit of your group.
- Prepare meticulously objectives, content, methods and styles, but be aware that that is not the whole answer.

- Spend time together, and familiarize yourselves with each other's strengths and shortcomings until you feel fine about them.
- Ask yourselves individually, and discuss together, why you are co-training? What are the advantages and drawbacks?
- Discuss in advance any difficulties you envisage could arise or concerns you have.
- Ask yourself and your co-trainer, 'Do I/you need to be a star?' Or do you both feel good enough about yourself and sufficiently trusting of each other to co-star?
- Decide in advance what you will do on the day if the partnership isn't working. How will you indicate this to each other?
- If you do end up on the sidelines, input as appropriate, but don't allow conflict to emerge between you during the session. The group will probably notice the lack of partnership between you, so there is no need for you to declare it.
- Try to talk to each other during a break, clarifying what you want done differently.
- If the 'single star show' goes on, don't try to compete, but make relevant contributions.
- Debrief fully afterwards, discussing your feelings, the effect it has had on you, what went wrong and why, and how you would like it to be.
- Give it another try, taking into account your mistakes and successes.
- Also know when to try and make it work and when it's time to say, 'I'm a good trainer, you're a good trainer, but not together'.
- Be sure to role model, and if you're teambuilding, work as a team, displaying true partnership.

In the lurch

Four weeks into the training my co-trainer said he didn't feel well and wasn't coming that day. The same thing happened the next week. The penny dropped: he wasn't coming back. I was left holding the baby.

This was compounded by having to deal with the negative feelings engendered in the group by his departure and the manner in which he left – no word of goodbye to the group, no message or explanation. What was his behaviour saying to a group that had agreed a set of ground rules which included commitment as a high priority?

I knew that my co-trainer had lacked confidence. On reflection, I could have helped matters by having more realistic expectations of his input. On his side, he could have been clearer with me about how he wanted us to work together. If he then felt the need to pull out, he had a responsibility to the group to say goodbye. As it was, I spent a lot of time debriefing feelings of confusion and uncertainty in the group and demonstrating my own commitment to the continuance of the training.

Role modelling co-training

A positive experience

One of my best memories of training is in partnership with another trainer. We were lead trainer and trainer, and we both knew and accepted that. That's what we wanted. We found a wonderful way of working together, planning in advance, consulting with each other in private and across the group. We were able to agree and disagree openly but constructively in front of the group. We could take mental breaks while staying alert. We never blamed each other when things went wrong, but used our debriefing sessions to encourage, review and suggest ways of improving each other's performance. On top of it all, we found a wonderful companionship.

Summary

We believe that whatever and however you are training or co-training, you must:

- motivate people to know what they know;
- build on their knowledge and use it;
- diagnose and influence others to diagnose;
- ask the right questions to make people think;
- listen and interpret;
- validate people's contributions;
- invite participation;
- focus and refocus people on the issue or new skills;
- encourage individual change and development;
- give advice and guidance; and
- impart new skills.

How do you do this?

In order to achieve these objectives, you have to:

- recognize your role as leader;
- inform yourself as much as possible before meeting a group;

- make no assumptions;
- understand the importance of group dynamics and its affect on learning;
- recognize and value your own particular expertise, and share it;
- give an opinion where appropriate even when people may not agree;
- give positive and negative feedback to create confidence and an opportunity for change; and
- learn from the participants so that you develop as a trainer.

Furthermore, when you are co-training you need to:

- share a common belief and approach;
- agree roles and input in detail beforehand;
- determine where the responsibility of each party begins and ends;
- discuss your differences in advance;
- decide how you will manage potential difficulties;
- have realistic expectations of each other;
- consult with each other before, during and after the sessions;
- use styles that may differ but that complement each other;
- accept that your co-trainer's style is different from yours;
- validate and encourage each other;
- develop a climate of trust where you can be honest about each other's shortcomings;
- role model in your partnership the principles you advocate for your participants;
- recognize that you as well as your co-trainer have responsibility for your part in any problems that arise as well as for resolving them;
- accept that participants may enjoy one trainer's style more than another and relate more easily to her or him.

3 The new trainer

The more I train, the more I learn

This chapter starts with trainers' memories of their first training sessions, and then, by means of a dialogue between an experienced trainer and a new trainer, we highlight some of the concerns you may have. The experienced trainer reflects on this conversation, recognizing the importance of keeping 'fresh eyes', so that you do not forget your earlier good practice when you took nothing for granted. Finally, there are some helpful hints for new trainers.

Starting out as a trainer

Memories of being new

I remember the first time I did some training. I spent hours preparing but I was so nervous I didn't know what to do. So, I talked all day – and everyone went to sleep. I couldn't understand it. It was snowing, so I opened the window in the afternoon. But they still went to sleep. I think they asked a few questions.

But I learnt from that experience when the person who had arranged the training took me to one side, and said, 'I think you're very good because you know your stuff, but I think you also need some training'. So I found myself a good trainer, and now I'm able to show others how to do it.

Learning on the job

Finding yourself training without having had any training yourself is a common experience. A trainer described how her managing director said:

'Come in on Tuesday and watch me do it and then you can do it on Thursday.' She did it with the notes, enjoyed it, and, as she thought, it was quite successful, but she describes her gradual understanding of her role as a trainer:

> They chose our company to do the training because of our good repu-
> tation and they liked our approach to the work. So I went there thinking:
> 'We know how to do it, I've got a good record and now I'll tell them how
> to do it. Simple.'
>
> I was arrogant, partly because I was young, I think. I didn't allow for
> any questions, probably because I was actually fearful. I must have
> appeared both unfeeling and bureaucratic. I know they didn't like me. I
> realized very quickly that this was not the right approach. Their situation
> was different from mine. Some of them were the victims of a changing
> political situation and they saw me as just one more harbinger of doom.

Her attitude changed, she says, to one of humility. She realized that life – or training – is not a battle to be fought and won:

> Once they began to talk to me, I became more sympathetic and under-
> standing. I learnt that the more we share, the more we benefit. I realized
> that everyone's frightened at times and we all have good and bad days.
> I didn't have absolute wisdom but I had ideas and experience to give.
> They needed to add their ideas to mine. I asked people for feedback,
> to elaborate on their experience. I asked for their thoughts and led them
> on. You are there to draw the best out of people; to find their strengths
> to do the task in hand; to tap into their intelligence, willpower, desire to
> achieve. They are there to have a good time, but also to benefit as
> much as possible from the training. I see my training quite differently
> now. I am, I think, a motivational speaker and a mediator of knowledge.

Early fears

Are you a new trainer stepping out for the first time? Do you hold onto your notes, worried about deviating from your planned programme but excited as the group responds to your ideas? Or, having trained for years, are you able to offer a well-structured session, even when you have for-gotten your notes, because you have done it so many times before? As an 'old' trainer, it's useful to remember those days when you did not take anything for granted, when, because you were new, you were also fresh.

To a new trainer every event is unexpected, because you have no previous experience to compare it with. You have not had the advantage of learning from your errors. This is the time when you make mistakes, but can also learn from them.

After training for years, it's easy to forget 'first night' nerves, the fear that you would forget your opening lines, that your trainees would see through you, and that punishing belief that 'all other trainers are better than me'! For the new trainer, however, having presented to the best of your ability, it can be quite devastating when some clever trainee pipes up with the last words you want to hear, 'It's obvious you're new to this'. The earth moves from under your feet, and you want to disappear.

The fears of the new and fairly new trainer are very real. As you present yourself to individuals who are vesting their trust and hopes in you, you may be busy finding your feet and coping with multiple self-doubts.

In conversation

A trainer, about to embark on her first training assignment, sought my advice. Our discussion revolved around the theme of personal development training.

OLD: How do you feel about your first course?

NEW: Terrified.

OLD: Why terrified?

NEW: Not knowing what to expect.

OLD: In time you'll learn to live with that. As you gain confidence as a trainer, this 'not knowing' is the very thing to make your adrenalin run. When you've presented the content many times before, you need something new to inspire you. The unpredictability of human nature stops the boredom.

NEW: Right now I'd feel better if I had some idea about the participants.

OLD: You could talk to them one by one before the course, face to face or on the phone. It'll be time consuming but worthwhile if you'll feel more at ease as a result. Make a check list first of what you want to find out from them.

NEW: Is there anything I must guard against?

OLD: Yes. Don't refer in the group to something an individual has told you in private. And don't assume that because someone has told you in private how they feel about the training or how they behave in groups, that they will feel or behave that way. You never really know until the group starts.

NEW: So would you recommend I speak to them first?

OLD: Do whatever is going to help you feel good and train well at this stage. My guess is that after a few training sessions the need to know in advance will disappear. When you're doing a lot of training it would be too much to take on. If you're doing something like team-building, it's a different matter. Pre-course interviews can be part of putting the training content and objectives together.

NEW: How much do you like to know before a course?

OLD: The names and job titles of participants gives me some of the picture. I discuss objectives and content with the Training Manager and/or the Departmental Manager when I'm training a department. Occasionally I write to the participants in advance, like with time management when I write to introduce myself and to ask them to do pre-course preparation. With stress management I might ask each individual to send me a brief outline of a stress they're experiencing. It helps me make the course relevant to them. However, I've also been led up the wrong path by it – by the time the course comes, they may want to do something completely different. Mostly, though, you don't have the chance to contact the participants beforehand. Some of them don't even know they're booked on the course until the day.

NEW: Is there anything I must know beforehand?

OLD: Timing. Start and finishing times, breaks and lunch. If refreshments are provided, whether they have to fetch them, or if they're brought to you. How many participants to expect. You can set your own maximum number. If possible, find out whether participants have chosen to come or been sent. Have they ever done training before. The course objectives, so that you can design the course. Talk to the relevant manager. Participants will also tell you their course expectations too at the start. Some of these expectations will coincide, others may even conflict with their manager's. I like to know if staff and their line manager are on the same course, as both can feel inhibited by this proximity. It will give you an idea of how freely people can speak.

NEW: How will I make sure that everyone works together?

OLD: Make a group contract. Find out what everyone needs in order to make it an open and safe learning environment.

NEW: What form of words shall I use? Shall I say that we're going to make a contract to ensure no *harm* comes to anyone during or after the session?

OLD: Some words are best avoided, and 'harm' is one of them. It will ring alarm bells. You'll sow the idea that they could be harmed. Find more positive words. Use words like 'concerns' instead of 'fear' or 'problem', 'preparation' and not 'homework', which reminds people of school. I use 'practising', not 'role play', since many people find the prospect of role play daunting.

NEW: What if they're all shy and quiet?

OLD: People are often shy at the start. Silences are fine, and not unusual. You don't have to fill them. They give everyone time to think, and shy people time to gather courage to speak.

NEW: Suppose they don't have views about the contract?

OLD: Write on the flipchart the main points you want. Explain them. Ask what else they want.

NEW: How do I get them talking more?

OLD: Start them off in pairs or threes with something easy, like 'What do you want from the course?' If people are nervous, they can talk to each other about it. Pairs are less threatening than the big group and threes can be easier than pairs, more dynamic. People sometimes get stuck in a pair, or don't get on together. Any other concerns?

NEW: Yes, about time. Will I have enough? How can I judge that?

OLD: I write down on my plans exactly how long I expect each activity to take overall, and each element of it. You can never tell precisely how long things will take – one group will want longer on a topic, another less. You must never waste people's time, so you learn to be responsive. You worry about timing less as you become more experienced, but planning keeps you on track, and stops you digressing.

NEW: Suppose I have too much time and not enough material?

OLD: Unlikely. In my experience there's never enough time. Occasionally you encounter a group who rush through the material. If they're very young, teenagers for example, and don't have such a range of experience to discuss, or they're new to training and unused to analysing their work, discussing issues or personal experience. Make sure you have extra material with you as a fallback. Anyway, I hope your first session goes well. Give me a ring and let me know.

[The phone call comes that evening]

OLD: How did it go?

NEW: It was my worst nightmare, though I feel better now.

OLD: Then tell me about the nightmare when we meet, if it can wait. Is there anything pressing?

NEW: I'm not sure what to do. I forgot to set the homework. Shall I ring them all?

OLD: Homework? Remember what I said about *homework*. Do you mean preparing for the next session?

NEW: Yes.

OLD: Do they really need to prepare before, I wonder? It strikes me that you could be setting yourself up if you ring between sessions. You might appear forgetful or disorganized. Worse still, they might gain the impression that you're available for advice between sessions. You could be on the phone for hours. However, if it's that important and there's a course administrator, ask them to send out a letter which you'll draft. You could say how pleased you were to meet them and you're looking forward to working with them over the coming weeks. Would they please *prepare* the following ... Alternatively, make the preparation a part of the first activity next week. They won't know you forgot to give them something, unless you tell them. You could end up doing that anyway, even if you speak or write in advance. People often forget to do preparation.

[*Meeting – after session one*]

OLD: You called it a *nightmare*? What would be your worst nightmare?

NEW: That I'd go blank when I'm standing up in front of everyone. Actually, that didn't happen, but I wasn't very clear. I didn't do what I told them I'd do.

OLD: Why did you call the first hour a *nightmare*?

NEW: Everything went wrong. I knocked over a cup of coffee. People arrived in dribs and drabs, which I hadn't considered and then they sat in stony silence waiting for latecomers. We were doing the first exercise, which seemed simple enough to me, when a woman burst into tears.

OLD: Anything, with hindsight, you could have done differently?

NEW: Not put coffee on the desk with my notes. Put information and a course outline on the seats for people to look at on arrival. Written an exercise on the flipchart asking them to introduce themselves to someone they haven't met before . . . I'm not sure how best to handle the tears.

OLD: It's important to complete the preliminaries early on. When participants start dribbling in, be ready for them. Have your coffee before they arrive. Give them your full attention. Go over and greet each person individually, welcome them warmly. Suggest they introduce themselves to people they don't know. They can then decide if they want to or not. If necessary, as it's the first day, tell them you'll start late as you're waiting for people to arrive. Give them the precise time. Say you'll start promptly in future. Repeat this when everyone has arrived. Incidentally, I like your idea about putting up a simple exercise on the flipchart.

NEW: What about the woman in tears?

OLD: People do cry occasionally, and I agree it's unfortunate when this happens right at the start. The whole group can be affected. It's different when they've met and talked to each other, and feel less inhibited about giving each other help and support. On the other hand, the group might develop an empathy. As the trainer, your role is to help them feel wanted and welcome. Someone who bursts into tears just as they're introducing themselves might feel embarrassed, guilty, even alone in the group. Say something like, 'I'm very glad you're here. Don't worry, it's fine to cry.' Check with them that it's all right to move on. Don't allow yourself to be drawn too much into their agenda – you're there for all the group, not just for the most fragile. You can always take them aside later and ask them in private how they are. Offer them time later to talk if they want to. How do you feel about the way you handled the process?

NEW: Fine, on the whole. I did have problems taking the group's feedback exercises. I hadn't thought about how to do that. I'd put them into four groups to discuss what they wanted from the course. Then I asked them in plenary and wrote their ideas on a flipchart. It took forever, and a couple of them said, 'Why can't we move on? We want to start.'

OLD: How did you respond?

NEW: I said, 'I'm aware it's time consuming, but it's most important for me to be aware of your expectations, so that we can try to meet them together.'

OLD: You handled that situation as well as any experienced trainer. It *is* important to take feedback regularly, but without spending too long over it. There are many different ways of taking feedback. You could ask them to discuss an issue and write the key points on the flipchart themselves. In case they want to 'censor' something, like a comment about a colleague, inform them that they'll be displaying the flips in plenary. Tell them to display the flips, ask for any comments, and add your own. Then their original ideas and words are a record to refer to during and after the course. Well, how do you feel about training now?

NEW: More confident but still nervous. Standing up there training terrifies me. As I stood there about to begin, I could hear myself thinking: 'Why am I doing this to myself?' If I panic, I go red for the whole group to see. My nerves are on full display. Right now I often go red. Things don't come naturally, because they're unfamiliar. I have to concentrate hard on the content.

OLD: That's not surprising. When you've done the content many times, it will flow. You'll be able to concentrate more on the process. Go with what you know. Your group will be engaged. It's all new to them. Once you feel fine with what you're doing now it's easier to introduce new material. How did you cope with your nervousness?

NEW: Head on. I told the group, 'I'm feeling quite nervous'. After that I felt calmer. I think they did too. They could see I was human.

OLD: Sounds as if you handled it well. An excellent piece of role modelling. However, a word of warning. It won't work with every group. Some could tease and give you a hard time. It's best not to reveal nerves too soon. The group could become nervous, and wary of placing their trust in you. When you see they're settling down, say something like 'I'm feeling more relaxed now too. I was rather nervous before.'

Over the next few weeks of the course the new trainer called me less, and the calls were shorter. She was finding her feet and gaining the confidence to answer her own queries. When the sessions were over, I rang to see how she had fared.

OLD: How did it go?

NEW: Very well. They wanted more, though I received some negative feedback too. They said it was too rushed, too packed.

OLD: That they wanted more is quite an achievement. Next time, remember that you don't have to do it all in one bite.

NEW: I realize that now. They need more time to digest the learning. I found it tiring too, all that energy on putting it together, dealing with their emotions and mine, and so on.

OLD: Training takes a lot out of you, no matter whether you're new or experienced [*see Chapter 6*]. But you do sound different now from the day before you started. What do you think?

NEW: Yes, I'm much more confident now, and pleased how things went. A little relieved it's over, though, until the next time . . .

OLD: That's how I feel . . . still . . . There's always the same anxiety about meeting a new group, and that's what keeps you on your mettle.

Although the new trainer came for advice, the old trainer found herself analysing the way she trained and learning a lot from the discussion.

Reflections on our conversation

At the end of the discussion I was reminded what it was like to be new, and how much I now take for granted.

> My notes, my notes, my kingdom for . . .
> One thing I do recall vividly: as a new trainer I was petrified to let go of my script. A far cry from now, when, in response to immediate needs, I can be spontaneous and cover topics I had not planned for. As a new trainer I wasn't familiar enough with the material to perform without my lines or to improvise. I needed then to work within a framework where I felt secure, so that the group did too. I was fine, as long as I didn't draw my newness to their attention, a surefire recipe for someone to exploit my vulnerability.

Now the worries are different.

I've heard this before

> I hear myself saying and thinking, 'Surely they've heard this before'. Of course, they haven't, but I have, frequently, because I've said it at so many courses. Sometimes I can't quite believe that the content is new to my latest group. If it's become boring for me or I don't find my own jokes funny any more, I find myself wondering what it must be like for them.

I have to remind myself not to take short cuts because I'm so familiar with the material. Recalling those days when I prepared for every minute of every session is a useful exercise. The challenge of experience is different from being new, but it is nevertheless still there. I manage it by the following means:

- I recognize that the material I'm offering is sound and interesting, but I use it differently so it is stimulating for me. I develop new exercises and activities, but I also make sure that I'm not missing out the key points just because I've heard them so often.
- I give myself 'dares' to do things differently. These keep me fresh and engrossed in what we're doing. The participants can soon sense when a trainer is bored.
- I constantly research my subject, keeping myself up to date and, of

course, developing my own learning. Expanding my knowledge can only be of benefit to the participants. However, when my latest interest or 'hobby horse' is not directly connected with what they want from the course, I have to be careful not to impose it on them.

When I was new to training, I thought all my troubles would go away as I became more experienced. They didn't, but they changed and gained in complexity. I created more challenges for myself, set myself higher standards, and others now have higher expectations of me. In turn, I am more spontaneous, more able to fine-tune training to organizational and individual needs. I cannot stress too much the importance of not becoming complacent, however experienced we may be as trainers. There is always something left to learn, especially from participants. I still consult books such as this, for many issues faced by old – as well as new – trainers are dealt with throughout. I still turn to colleagues to ask for help or advice. I consider supervision and mentoring invaluable, whether you're just starting off or simply trying to stay fresh.

Summary

Here are some hints to start you off on the right foot:

- Clarify with the administrative staff beforehand how you want the room laid out.
- Check all the equipment in advance.
- Give the group practical details at the start, such as where to find toilets and fire escapes.
- Look at each individual in your group. Don't miss anyone out, or they will feel left out.
- Use clear, dark-coloured flipchart pens, like black and blue. Some people have difficulty distinguishing red and green. Ask if everyone can see what you write on the flipchart.
- At the outset make an agreement of confidentiality to protect the participants and clarify what confidentiality means, namely that (a) You are not there on behalf of management or to report back personally on individual participants; and (b) they can take content and issues back to the workplace, but not someone else's personal information or viewpoint.
- Write the exact words participants use on the flipchart. Don't rephrase or redefine what they say, but make sure you value their words. If something is unclear, ask what they mean, or solicit an example.

- When you set an exercise requiring participants to write on the flip-chart, ask them to do likewise (i.e. write down the exact words used without rephrasing or redefining).
- Tell participants that there are no marks for spelling whenever they write (i.e. they need not be embarrassed to write in front of others).
- As a trainer, presumably you can spell and, if not, at least ensure that you have learned the key words (e.g. 'role' play, not 'roll' play)!
- When you set exercises, do not assume that everyone will hear your instructions the first time you say them. Someone may well ask, right in the middle of an exercise, 'What are we supposed to be doing?'
- Check that people know what they are doing. Wander from group to group, hovering at an appropriate distance. Notice what is going on without intruding, unless they call you or you identify the need to intervene.
- Verify the timing of each exercise, saying how long they have. If they are really involved in the exercise, judge whether to allow longer than the time you originally allotted and check if they need more time.
- Notice if one group finishes long before the rest. Have fallback topics for them to discuss that are related to the exercise.
- Leave yourself and the group time for a proper ending. For example, you might do the evaluations, then have a quarter of an hour for a closing exercise. Better to round off than to rush off.

4 Who's directing?

It made it all worthwhile when the director said, 'This training has really turned things around'.

In this chapter, we investigate who actually establishes the training needs, who decides on the training, and how you, the trainer become involved. We highlight the importance of developing a good working relationship with the 'director' by recognizing and establishing each others' responsibilities and negotiating how you do things together.

In the training room

Training can be subversive. You are asking people to think differently and generate ideas. Participants take ideas back into the workplace. They may ask questions or ask for changes. How much of this is your responsibility? How much should the organization expect this to happen after the training?

As an in-house trainer, you can find yourself too closely identified with the organization or at odds with what is going on. There are constraints if, as one put it, you 'have to dance to the organisation's tune'. On the other hand, you may be expected to work miracles or resolve major problems. You fully understand the working context and you must be realistic.

External trainers may have left an organization because they wanted more autonomy and independence. But you can find yourself 'belonging' to an organization just for a day. What happens if you do not agree with its policies and procedures? As an external trainer you do not necessarily have to toe the party line, but you do have to be aware of how the organization works. If you don't, you can make it very difficult for the participants, raising unreal expectations or fomenting discontent.

You may feel you are out there alone, but unless you have put on the course yourself, there is usually a 'director' behind you.

Getting the work

How do you get the work? Is it your reputation? Is it competitive tendering? Are you the designated training officer? Who chose you?

Your first contact with the director can range from the formal interview or presentation as part of the tendering process, a fairly informal discussion with a manager, or a phone call asking you to turn up with your material on a certain day. On the other hand, you may be well known in the organization: you are in the training department, a tried and trusted trainer, or you have been previously involved in establishing the organization's training needs.

The director can help or hinder the training process, and the role varies enormously. For example, he or she may be the head of a large human resources department, the director of a tiny voluntary organization, the manager of a small section, or the training administrator who has been asked to ring you up, to name but a few of the possible guises.

First meetings

As trainer, you are managing a multitude of demands: from the organization, from the people setting up the training, and from the participants themselves. You have to balance all these demands and bring an objective eye to what is needed.

Even if the director sees herself or himself as merely the purchaser and leaves the rest to you, it is still worth doing some research on what is really needed. Trainers can be called in to do work which participants find entirely irrelevant to their needs, which is not fair either on them or on you. If the location is not too far away, arrange a meeting with the director. Emphasize the importance of the working relationship by saying something along the following lines: 'I like to see who I'm working for before I start and find out about your organization. I think it's also extremely important that you see me and find out if I'm the sort of person you want.'

Sometimes it is possible to meet the participants beforehand too. Trainers called in to do teambuilding, for example, find it useful to meet individuals and research the situation before meeting as a group. Participants can also turn into directors – directing from the floor, changing the agenda, wanting you to address their particular needs – so the more you know about them from the outset, the better.

Some directors want to be fully involved in designing and developing the training. There can be a problem when the 'director' is also a trainer and finds it hard to delegate to you, or when she or he takes on the role of boss:

> I obtained the work through a tender and received an enormous contract to read. Then the head of training invited me in for an 'informal' meeting. He proceeded to give me a lecture on how I should train, what I could and couldn't do, even down to telling me what sort of clothes I was expected to wear. I know they want high standards, but after going through the tendering process, I felt as if he was questioning my reputation and integrity. As you can imagine, I felt like dropping the training there and then, but I took it on. I have managed to develop a reasonable working relationship, but I still don't find it easy to go and discuss the training afterwards. It's a pity because we're all missing out in this situation, the delegates included.

There may also be difficulties in communication and decision-making when the director, or in this case the training department, is contracting on behalf of someone else, or if their main concern is making a profit:

> They kept everything to themselves. I wanted to find out the participants' needs as I felt the training was being imposed on them. But they wouldn't let me talk to the manager. They said they were arranging the training and that was their job. I knew it was because they were basically subcontracting and they were terrified I'd take their business away.

Some training departments are suspicious of outsiders or have been left with a bad impression by trainers who have undercut them or taken work away from them.

Providing equality of opportunities

The director may ask you, and expect you, to sign a contract committing yourself to observe the organization's Equal Opportunities policy and practice, and to translate this into action. You will, of course, want to take account of this policy and practice if you are training in equal opportunities, but it is applicable to every topic, for example, information technology, or writing and meetings skills.

The director may provide you with a detailed code of practice specifying what you do, and how you communicate. She or he may even be prescriptive, stating which language and words to use, and which to avoid. Some trainers provide a clear written statement of intent before the course showing how their commitment to policy is matched by practice. This includes:

- Asking for the client's policy at the beginning of the working relationship, and finding out their procedures for equal opportunities.
- Reviewing the work regularly with the client and with an outside supervisor.
- Designing programmes where all participants can value their own experience and feel confident to contribute.
- Setting a contract for working at the beginning of all courses which includes a commitment to equal opportunities.
- Checking the accessibility of the building, training room and resources for people with disabilities.
- Arranging to meet special individual requirements in advance and on the day, such as handouts in braille, cassettes or engaging signers.
- Being sensitive about choice of words and language while not allowing it to place adverse constraints on the training.
- Ensuring that discriminatory terms or assumptions are not used in oral presentations, discussions and written materials.
- Ensuring that visual images reflect diversity.
- Supporting and encouraging participants (a) to recognize and (b) to challenge discrimination.
- Asking for written and spoken evaluation from participants about the training and consultancy carried out.
- Designing programmes which take into account people's individual needs and requirements as well as those of the group.

Discrimination takes place when someone is treated less favourably than another on grounds of gender, marital status, sexual orientation, ethnic origin, colour, disability, age, class, creed, religion or political activity. Indirect discrimination can take place when assumptions are made about individuals, or unjustifiable conditions or requirements imposed which exclude groups of people. As a trainer you may have considerable power when you are alone working with your group and are therefore in a position to discriminate directly as well as indirectly. You need to be continually alert to the impact of your training and your behaviour on groups and individuals.

Getting to know each other

The closer the partnership between the director and you, the better the training. Good directors:

- give you relevant background knowledge of the organization or department;
- understand why the course is required;
- have thought out the objectives and how they fit into the overall training plan;
- know the participants' training needs; and
- understand your role in this project.

They have much to lose if they contract the wrong trainer, as this director describes:

> At the first meeting it's more important to me that the trainer shows interest in the organization and how we work before she or he starts telling me how they are going to do the training. I don't like it when they come in like sales people. I look for empathy, someone who is interested in people and wants to understand how what they offer can fit in with what we do here. Coupled with this I want someone who can develop and deliver clear, relevant training.

The director therefore wants information about you. Most people ask for written information, but even if they don't, it's a good idea to give them some. Whether you do it verbally or in writing, you need to:

- give some background about yourself;
- show your previous experience;
- list who else you have worked with;
- show what you can offer;
- demonstrate your knowledge of their field (You don't necessarily have to have been a banker to train in a bank, but you do want to show that your knowledge and experience, is applicable, say, to working on interpersonal skills or recruitment.);
- describe your training methods; and
- tell them how you think you can help their organization.

Finally, you have a responsibility to consider the following questions:

- Am I the right person to run the course?
- Can I offer relevant skills and experience or develop these to run a new course?
- Will my training style and philosophy be appropriate for this course and organization?
- Am I prepared to commit my time to this training?

Planning together

If you, the director and the participants are all agreed about the direction of the training beforehand, you will be able to design a programme which takes into account the organizational and individual needs. An in-house trainer describes how the training has improved since the managers have become involved with planning the programmes:

> I often felt I was working in a vacuum before, but now the managers are leading the training programme. They are aware of their staff needs through appraisal. We discuss and plan the programme together. They leave it up to me to plan the content and methodology. But they also follow it up afterwards.

Her experience is very different from the trainer's below:

> I go into some places, do the training and walk out at the end feeling I could say, 'That's it, I've serviced the boiler, I'm going now', and no one would notice. It's one thing valuing your autonomy as an independent trainer, but it's another believing that the organization values what you're doing and is likely to do some follow-up.

Some directors do not have a very clear idea of what is needed, and therefore appreciate the opportunity to establish with you what is relevant and how staff could benefit from your training. They may leave most of the planning to you, but you must still check with them and let them see your programme beforehand, so that they have an opportunity to suggest any changes.

Where you have a very directive director, you will have to negotiate some flexibility or you will feel that you are in a straitjacket. Some trainers write in clauses when submitting their programmes, such as:

> The content will be covered, but not necessarily in this order

or

> While I aim to meet the course objectives, as the trainer I reserve the right to flexibility according to identified needs of individuals and the group.

You may do all this planning with one person who is not actually going to be at your session, so you must also bear in mind that you are planning for others. The clearer the director is about who the participants are and what their training needs are, the more relevant your training will be to them. You want therefore to find out from the director:

- What relationship does the director have with participants?
- Does she or he meet with the participants beforehand, or is she or he solely a training organizer?
- How else does she or he assess the training needs?
- What does the organization want to achieve through the training?
- Is this a one-off programme? If it is, what are they wanting out of it?
- Is the training primarily for the participants' personal development and learning, or is it part of an overall strategy in the organization to improve the quality?
- How much is the director committed to following up the training?
- How will the course be evaluated and what criteria does the director use to judge success?
- How does she or he see and value the training?
- What scope does she or he give you for being creative?

Customer care

The relationship between the director and you, the trainer, is a crucial if delicate one, whether you are an in-house or independent trainer. Developing a trusting relationship with your director is one of the rewards of training, particularly if you come in from outside. It relieves some of the loneliness of the job. You have someone to explore ideas with, someone who supports you and is there to talk through the training when it is finished. It is also of enormous benefit to the trainees. After all, they are all your customers.

You can put on a superb course which benefits the participants considerably, but if it is underpinned by the agreed values and expectations of the director and the organization, it will be even more worthwhile.

Summary

Whoever you are working with, make sure that you are *both* clear about your differing roles:

- Find out why you have been asked in, and what expectations the organization has of both you and the training.

- Clarify your responsibilities and who organizes what.
- Decide together who makes decisions. You suggest the training process, but the director may want some say in the content. You need to clarify how this fits into the plan and whether you are in agreement.
- Find out if there are 'house rules' or styles to which you or participants are expected to conform.
- Ask for the background of the participants and how they are chosen for the course. Suggest, if this has not already been done, that participants fill up a pre-course questionnaire so you know whether their objectives fit in with yours and with those of the training organization.
- Make sure you have clarified and agreed the aim of the course with the director before you embark on it. Discuss differences and negotiate.
- If you are being paid as an external trainer, make sure you have agreed the terms before the training starts. Be clear what you charge, and whether you are prepared to negotiate, and be up front about it. In some sectors, it is new for directors to have to talk money. Some trainers are much more confident about asking for money than others. If you have difficulty:
  - (a) find out what the going rate is in the sector in which you are working;
  - (b) talk to other trainers about what they charge; and
  - (c) charge a fee which you feel comfortable with, so that you are neither resentful because you feel you are being asked to do something on the cheap, nor burdened with undue pressure because you have asked for such a high fee.

  Good training is valuable. If you have something good to offer and don't exploit your clients, you are sure to be asked back for more.
- Check through any contract you have to sign, looking carefully at the terms and conditions. If you are not clear what is meant on any point, ask, and discuss at the outset anything you can not agree on.

5 The fragile trainer

Even in a crisis I keep my professional hat firmly on my head.

We discovered as we discussed this book together that we both had anxieties as trainers, but that they took different forms. One of us does all her worrying beforehand and not during the training. The other sleeps well the night before but worries during the session. We are not suggesting that either way is right or wrong – it is just how we are.

In this chapter we illustrate how even experienced and successful trainers may be coping with personal anxieties and external pressures as they work. They may even be placing some of these pressures on themselves. We have found that acknowledging and discussing such pressures with others helps you to live with and manage them.

What's going on in your life?

The pressure to be a role model to your participants on every occasion can be a strain. On top of all that, you have to contend with whatever else is going on in your life, like the times when you don't sleep at night, feel unwell or have had a row before leaving for work. You may be struggling with the pain of a broken relationship, or the anguish of illness and death in the family. Will you be able to cope?

Sleepless nights

Do you ever have sleepless nights before you train? They may occur when you:

- are new to training;

- have an unfamiliar journey;
- work with a new client or client group;
- expect the training to be problematic; and/or
- are dealing with your own emotional strains.

> I couldn't sleep the night before – partly excitement, partly worry. My adrenalin was racing 24 hours ahead. I'd fall into a deep sleep around 6 a.m. only to wake with the alarm at 7 a.m., feeling sick and wobbly.

A new trainer may find this a common experience; the pattern changes with time. But if it persists, think about breaking this habit before it saps your strength and mental acuity.

GUIDELINES

- Keep a reuseable checklist of items you need, personally and for training.
- Familiarize yourself with the course content.
- Set a deadline for preparing and know when you have done enough.
- Take exercise.
- Eat early and light.
- Ensure that everything is ready before going to bed.
- Try not to refer to your notes again after completing your preparation.
- Relax – watch the television, meet friends, go to the cinema.
- Do relaxation exercises before bed – perchance to sleep.

Even if you still cannot sleep, you will probably be fine. Adrenalin, your worst enemy at night, is your friend by day; it's the hormone that helps you to cope under stress. You may need less sleep than you think. You can always catch up on it later.

Worrying about the journey

Worrying about the journey or an unfamiliar training location may override your concerns about the training itself. Will you lose your way, will you be late? Will you rely on public transport? The train might break down. Will you drive? What if there's a traffic jam, or nowhere to park? What a bad impression you'll give if you're late: unreliable and stressed. How will you regain the confidence of the group if you set off on the wrong foot? And will you be able to find things when you arrive – the room, staff, resources? Will you be able to operate the equipment?

> One freelance trainer who works in umpteen venues still worries about

her journeys. 'I worry every time I go somewhere new. Once I've been there a few times, I'm fine. My problem is coping with the unknown. I need routine and a sense of belonging. I've found that having a pre-meeting with the organization and visiting the training room in advance greatly reduces my anxiety.'

GUIDELINES

- Wherever possible have a pre-meeting to: discuss needs, content, resources and break times; see the room and check out the equipment and facilities; meet the participants (when feasible); and find out about public transport and parking.
- You may want to do the journey once before the training date to see the location and estimate the journey time.
- Plan to arrive 30 minutes to an hour early, allowing for unexpected crises like security alerts and diversions.
- Bring your contact's name and telephone number.
- If you carry a mobile phone, have a full battery – and call if you're running late.
- Ensure they have got your phone number.

On the edge of a precipice

Some circumstances may result in your feeling very fragile, such as sickness, emotional upset, discord, a broken relationship, or grief from the loss of a loved one.

Feeling ill

However fit you are now, you could feel ill one day. As luck will have it, it is bound to happen before a special day's training where your expectations, and everyone else's, are high.

A solo freelance trainer was due to run a pilot session that could lead to a mammoth contract. The day before, he suddenly developed stomach pains and nausea. He described his dilemma:

I toyed with the idea of finding a substitute in case I still felt bad the next day. But then they'd need time to prepare. They might let me down – not turning up or doing a bad job. Worse, they might be so good that I'd lose my client to them. I worried about saying I was sick at all, in case my client saw me as a risky prospect who might not turn up on the day. I gave myself a hard time, yet I hadn't pulled out of training through illness for five years – a first-class record.'

In this situation you have several options.

GUIDELINES

- Accept that you do not have to be superhuman just because you are a trainer.
- Deal with the immediate situation by being honest; stating that you are disappointed but sick and unable to train. Convey apologies to the participants and ask to rearrange the date. Confirm both apologies and new date in writing.
- Write to the participants explaining that you are ill, and that you look forward to seeing them on the rearranged date.
- Develop ongoing arrangements with trusted colleagues who could substitute at short notice, or be on standby for any training arranged on future dates.
- Inform the client in advance that you can arrange a substitute to cover in the unlikely event of your being unable to train.
- Make arrangements for direct invoicing to yourself so that you pay the substitute and thus preserve your personal relationship with the client.

Breaking up is hard to do

I had just started as a trainer when unexpectedly the relationship with my long-term partner broke up. I was very distressed and suffering from shock. Ironically I was in the middle of a series of courses on improving communication skills. At home, I spent a lot of time drifting about and crying. Yet immediately I reached the venue, I set about my work. I don't know how I did it, but the great thing about being the trainer is that you have to concentrate. People are looking to you. I think it's different if you're a participant.

Each morning I literally put on my professional clothes, dressing carefully, putting my face straight, and gathering my props so that I could take on the role of trainer. I imagine actors feel like this – the show must go on. And it did. I went home each night and cried again, but not about the training. It went amazingly well, although I can't remember much about it now. I felt rejected by my partner, but being part of an accepting group, who knew nothing about me, helped a lot.

GUIDELINES

The trainer telling this story said that looking back on this period, she learnt:

- The importance of recognizing and holding on to your professional skills.
- How to use the trainer's role which gives you authority and therefore strength to get on with the job.
- How keeping your professional and personal life separate, even in moments of crisis helps everyone.
- To recognize her vulnerability, but not to bring her problem into the group.
- There are others outside to talk to and lean on.
- To allow herself time for her distress outside, but to concentrate totally on the job while training.

You are expected to have, and indeed need, enormous reserves as a trainer, and you can usually find them, even when they're buried deep. Other trainers have commented how, in similar personal crises, they have sometimes done some of their best work. They suggest that this is due to being unable to take anything for granted as you make an extra effort to concentrate and to being sensitized by your own circumstances. Since your life has been turned upside down you have to reassess what is going on, and this has an impact on the training.

Loss and bereavement

> Above all I feared losing someone I loved, with the prospect of having to stand in front of a group, outwardly confident, inwardly grieving. And then it happened. In the middle of a very busy period, I learned that my mother had cancer, and had only a short time to live. Caring for her while she suffered and deteriorated, I wondered how I would cope once I'd lost my dearest friend and adviser.
>
> I thought that I wouldn't cope, and yet I discovered that I had reserves of strength I didn't know existed. The fear that I would 'collapse in a trembling heap' was not borne out and I attributed much to my own stability and the way that I handled the crisis. I grieved, talked, took a break, returning to work when I felt ready. I recognized I'd be ready for different areas of my work at different stages. I needed to pace myself and not feel guilty about saying to clients: 'I haven't done this yet. I've had a bereavement. I will do it before the end of the month.'

GUIDELINES

- When you learn that someone you love is ill, put work second.
- Take time off to be 'yourself' and to be with them, so that you won't have to look back and say, 'If only I'd . . .'

- Give yourself time to grieve. Don't rush back to work through worry or the need to escape.
- Let people know how you feel. Ask for help and accept it when it is offered. Don't give people the impression that you are a person who can manage all on your own.
- Be aware that bereavement can cause not only the obvious side of grief, such as sudden tears and flood of emotion, but also physical exhaustion, low energy and loss of concentration. You may be able to concentrate on one thing, but not another. Listen to the demands of your body, and delegate, plan and pace yourself to take account of your new situation.
- See a bereavement counsellor. You may do much giving in your work and be unused to receiving, but now it's time for you to receive and to have time for yourself alone. Take that time. Talk through your concerns about how loss could affect your training. Determine how you can best take care of yourself, and do it.
- The next time you train, you may find it helpful to tell your group, 'I've recently had a bereavement', and then to move on.
- If you need it, take brief time out away from your group during an exercise.
- Set limits on what you do during the training. Know when to take a step back and say to yourself, 'This is good enough!'
- See your role as the trainer and not the grieving person.
- Expect that your professionalism will see you through – as hers did in the previous story.

Vulnerable and on the spot

There are times when you go ahead against your better judgement. There they are, the audience, waiting with bated breath and eager-eyed for you, the trainer, source of all knowledge, tower of strength, healer, entertainer, answer to their problems! Only today *you* are feeling fragile!

No matter how professional you are, the worry is that human frailty will interpose – and when you least expect it. You suddenly feel violently sick, or a chance comment triggers a deep emotion. You fall to pieces, literally and metaphorically.

My best friend

My best friend died a week before I was due to present an important stress management course. I coped well at first and thought I was fine to train. Then it hit me. I wept buckets, for her, the family and the huge gap in my own life. I worried that I wouldn't have the strength or interest to facilitate others in learning to manage their stress at such a stressful and distressing point in my own life. I was terrified that I would burst into tears. And I did!

At the time, I felt that I had left it too late to pull out of the training. How could I ring them that same morning and say, 'I won't be there?' With hindsight I realize that I would have done better to do exactly that. I wasn't in a fit state to train at all that day. However inconvenient it would have been for the company, I think they would have understood. If they hadn't, I would not want to work for them anyway.

Toothless in the plaza

I was due to deliver a confidence and positive self-image course in a plush venue to a plush group of people. The previous evening my bridge, which had become rather wobbly, dropped out of my mouth. I had a large gap right at the front, and I looked almost threatening when I smiled. So much for role-modelling a positive self-image.

I decided honesty and lightness were my best friends. The next day I smiled broadly as I welcomed the group and said: 'I'm delighted to welcome you. I'm rather embarrassed as my front bridge decided to go for a walk last night. Now I'll ignore it. I trust you can too.'

It's all right for you

I was employed as a trainer in a large company that was in the throes of reorganization, and everyone was insecure. Then came my turn. I'd be out of a job in a month. I loved my work. I was shattered.

It was a poignant experience to go in the next day to train a group of staff all facing imminent redundancy. Keeping my own situation private, we were getting on with the session when someone told me, 'It's all right for you . . .' It was the last straw. I burst into tears.

At the time, I handled it well. I asked to be excused for a while so that I could recover myself. When I returned and explained why I'd burst into tears there was an immediate empathy in the group and it went brilliantly. But I can see now that it might have been better to disclose my situation right from the start.

What's going on in your head?

As if there's not enough to deal with externally, you may have inner fragilities too. Do you give yourself a hard time, want to be perfect, to be liked, to make it the best day's training the participants have ever had? Do you compare yourself unfavourably to the next trainer? Do you worry whether you will be asked back again?

Trainers who appear extremely confident admit to all sorts of fears that don't necessarily go away, so you may have to learn to live with them. These do not have to stop you being a good trainer. Indeed, they may well enhance your training. The degree of discomfort which we discuss in Chapter 2 prevents complacency. You become more attentive – you are 'human'. Groups observing the trainer's 'reserve' – or fragility – at the start of a course frequently find that it allows them time to settle in, acknowledge their own anxieties and open up – to be 'human' too.

It is when the negative messages or self-doubt intrude that you need to take action. So what sort of things do you say to yourself?

They'll find me out – do I really know more than them?

You may ask yourself this when working on new material or when the participants have a particular specialism that you don't have.

> I was asked to run an assertiveness course for a group of doctors. As I was preparing, the image of my GP giving me an injection and telling me to relax hung over me: she competent, knowledgeable – me, feeling ghastly, tearful and vulnerable. As I worked I began worrying about my lack of medical knowledge. I convinced myself that doctors would be 'experts' in assertiveness and I would have nothing new to say to them. I wasted hours of preparation time just worrying. Ten minutes into the training I realized that they were a highly motivated and interested group – a pleasure to work with. We were both expert in our respective fields.

GUIDELINES

From this experience I learnt:

- You do not have to know everything.
- Participants give you an 'authority' which you can gladly receive and use positively.
- Putting your own and the participants' expertise together creates a good learning situation.

It isn't working

> I never relax but spend the whole time worrying: Is the material all right? Have I judged the time correctly? Are the participants really benefiting from the training?

GUIDELINES

You can use this concern positively to:

- Be constantly alert to what is happening within the group.
- Evaluate as you go along.
- Let participants know that the programme can be flexible.
- Check with the participants whether an exercise has worked.
- Take risks and try out new exercises and materials. You will be worried anyway, whether it's new or old material!

I have to be perfect

Are you the person who has to print all the handouts because there is a smudge on them? Do you blame yourself when the course doesn't turn out as expected, or when people miss the key points?

High standards are one thing, but changing the attitudes of a group on a one-day course is another. Why do you have to be perfect when you are allowing participants to make mistakes, and even suggesting to them that mistakes are acceptable?

One trainer told us with an ironic smile:

> I give myself a hard time with my constant drive to be the perfect trainer. Yet if I see a participant driving him/herself into the ground, I'm in there asking, 'Why do you demand so much of yourself?' and 'Do you expect perfection from others one hundred percent of the time?' They could well ask the same of me.

Confidence crisis

> I've been training for years, yet for no apparent reason I suddenly lose confidence. For example, a course on managing change was going well. Rationally, I knew it, but emotionally I couldn't see it. At the end of the first day I told myself I hadn't picked up the main points, hadn't asked the right questions, had been unfocused. How could I go back for the second day? They'd think, 'What a waste of time, she's not very good'. I have to say, this was all in my head. The reality wasn't like that at all.

GUIDELINES

The trainer described how she managed this crisis. She realized:

- The middle of a course is often a low point. We've put our cards on the table, and there are both questions and ideas. The next step is to organize them so that they make sense.
- Participants may also feel that they are in the middle of something and uncertain what the ending will be. Endings are important to bring everything together and see what you have been doing as a whole.
- At the end of the first day check how participants feel about what they have done and where they want to go next. They will tell you if they think any points are not relevant.
- Crises of confidence are sometimes caused by a surge of adrenalin, but the course content can also make you anxious. Managing change, for instance, is an emotive subject. It touches both you and others, there are no pat answers, and, unlike some skills courses, you cannot wholly control the content.
- Participants are more relaxed on the second day. Start off positively and use their confidence to feed in to your own.

Thoughts on groups

I want them to like me

> I do find it difficult when people seem to dislike me for no apparent reason.

It's gratifying when warmth and friendliness flows from the group to you. The participants want to be with you, enjoy your company, think you're great. Yet most of us come up against people who don't like us. Sometimes, it is just that they don't like you as a person, in which case there is little you can do about that except get on with the job and not take it personally.

However, you also meet the hostile and angry participants whose behaviour has nothing to do with who you are or what you say. You can be the repository for all sorts of negative feelings. Here, honesty and integrity is the best policy. Even if they don't like you, they will usually respect you.

I don't like them

> Sometimes it's like walking into the lion's den. There are certain groups of workers that I dread. They're usually stressed and cynical. You can

see them thinking, 'So here's another of those overpaid trainers come to waste our time'.

GUIDELINES

A group like this is a real challenge. In such a situation:

- Focus on the material so that you are not drawn down into their feelings.
- Give everyone time to talk.
- Acknowledge that stress and cynicism exist.
- Find the positive people in the group and let their voices be heard.
- Don't think you have to provide solutions for everything.

I'm getting nowhere

I spent the whole day trying to persuade the group to move on. I felt that I was getting nowhere. The afternoon was particularly hard going and I blamed myself for not interesting them. It was only at the end that I realized that two key people in the group never spoke to each other at work. But the whole group had put on a show of solidarity: 'Everything is going well, there are no real problems,' they said. They either did not want, or were not ready, to acknowledge the real situation or indeed to change matters. I left disconsolate and feeling that somehow I had been in collusion with them.

There are bound to be groups who, like individuals, feel safer with the status quo, however unpleasant this is. In such circumstances, being isolated as a trainer can make you feel as if it is you that has failed the participants. You have to remind yourself that groups need to be part of the learning dynamic as well – you are not in the training room alone.

Training is not the answer to everything, and sometimes you may have to be content with having done a good day's work without obvious or great results.

I'm not part of the group

It's stupid really – I don't want to go to the pub with them, but, it can be quite disconcerting not to be invited, particularly as an in-house trainer. It's as if I don't belong to the same company.

Training on your own is a lonely business. Participants can create an intimacy together – particularly when they work in small groups. Even groups who did not know each other in the first place get to know things which you never learn. They will talk about you and judge you.

You can feel excluded when you are placed on a pedestal or seen as a person apart. Never being wholly part of the group, however, is where your strength lies. You have the capacity to remain outside and look in. How many times have you thought to yourself 'Yes, I've been there – I didn't recognize it then, but I can see it from this position'? Now you can distinguish the wood from the trees, and give sound advice and observations. In so doing, you may have to challenge, suggest change, point out the truth of what is happening. You don't have to be remote, but being an empathetic 'outsider' has definite advantages.

Summary

We believe that having and creating your own support is pivotal to being successful as a trainer and enjoying training.

Being a trainer, you could find that family, friends and colleagues think of you as the strong one among them – leader, guide, adviser, a shoulder to lean on. Therefore, when you are the one who feels fragile, they may find it hard to understand. It upsets their perception of you as the coper, and they may not quite know how to react.

Indeed, you may collude with that image of yourself, feeling that you ought to be strong and always able to cope. However, while you do have responsibilities to your participants when you are training, you also have a personal duty – a duty to take care of yourself and to acknowledge that you are also a human being.

Don't

- Think that as trainer and role model you have to be able to handle everything.
- Think that you 'should' be able to stand firm by yourself at all times.

Do

- Make life as easy for yourself as possible in order to manage the demands of training.
- Plan in advance and organize fallback arrangements to meet possible crises.
- Take comfort from the knowledge that the blood will likely rush to stimulate body and brain as soon as you take centre stage.

- Recognize that a professional hat is a powerful antidote when you're feeling fragile.
- Accept that it's human to be fragile sometimes.
- Build a support network around yourself, positive people you can trust – family, friend, colleague, training network, support organizations, regular supervision – and who you can turn to and call on for help when you need it.

When all's said and done, the show must go on – and it usually does! Only on rare occasions may the performance have to be put off to another day.

6 The weary trainer

It's difficult to say the same thing twenty times during the day and say it fresh each time.

An experienced trainer told me as I was starting out ten years ago: 'Make sure you look after yourself. You will need to do a great deal yourself.' I was rather shocked at this. It sounded selfish. I had always worked with people and felt I coped well. Why should this be any different?

It's an exhausting job being a trainer. Therefore, in this chapter we shall discuss ways of conserving your energy; keeping going; and pacing yourself.

Most trainers work on their own and this means you need a high degree of self-sufficiency, plus emotional and physical strength. From the moment you start the training, your concentration cannot waiver. The group literally looks to you – you lead, energize and keep the whole show going. People may dump their emotions – for example, distress, frustration anger – on you, but you have to control your own. They also bring with them high expectations. When you ask them what they want to achieve from the course they may joke, 'I want to change my life' or 'I want miracles', but there will probably be some truth in these statements. And you have to respond to all this, even if you don't accept it. Hence it is difficult for those who don't do this kind of work to fully understand when you come home and say, 'I'm knackered'.

As you become more experienced, you recover more quickly; you find ways of relaxing. There will still be times, however, when you will be exhausted by the sheer volume of training, the numbers of people you meet, and the kinds of problems and needs they bring. The physical and emotional demands catch up with you.

In looking after your participants, you can easily forget to look after yourself. To work well, you need refreshment – you may tell the participants this, but even if you are a star in stress management, you can fail to heed your own advice. Thus you need:

- to have physical stamina to stay the course;
- to be able to cope with the emotional demands of training; and
- to guarantee the balance between work and leisure.

Much of the time you will be able to do this. When, however, you suddenly find that your concentration is poor, your ideas have dried up, and that you lack stamina, feel drained and are easily irritated, these symptoms are all telling you that it's time to do something.

Conserving your energy

The night before

- Having everything ready the night before helps you to unwind. Several trainers said that they finish their preparations early, with a clear cut-off point before dinner and time to relax after it, otherwise they felt that they had no break between one day's work and the next and found it hard to sleep because of all the thoughts buzzing through their heads.
- The truly organized kept a check list on the wall above their desk, comprising everyday items needed for training. Some also kept a pre-packed bag of everyday 'tools of the job' like blue-tak, flip chart pens and notebooks, with other items pertaining to a particular course being packed the evening before (e.g. handouts, contact name and phone number, telephone number of venue and a map).

In the morning

- Being completely ready the night before clears the decks for early morning fresh air and exercise, if this suits you. Instead, or as well, have an unhurried breakfast rather than taking your toast on the bus or coffee in the car.

During the day

- On arrival, seek help to arrange things, rather than doing it all yourself – unless you prefer to. With luck the room will be set up already exactly as you specified in advance. Take steps to protect yourself. Make the ground rules work for you, as well as for your group: for example, ask them to respect your break times. Explain that you may separate yourself from them for part or all of the break(s), as you will want some 'space' during the day (i.e. to relax, to think, to review). Advance explanations pre-empt having to deal with or refuse participants' queries at such times. If you do sit with them at lunch, talk about matters unconnected with the course. Remind them of the ground rule if they disturb your break, and arrange a time to talk to them later.

● Conserve and raise your energy levels. Avoid extra meetings on a training day, conserving all your energy for the task in hand. Use active exercises to refresh you and your participants throughout the day, and trust that your adrenalin will see you through.

You can plan for all these factors and take steps to control them. However, other issues, circumstances and personalities can affect the way that you feel both during and outside training.

Keeping going – during training

The drains

Although you are tired, you meet groups from time to time who carry you through – such is their enthusiasm, humour and thoughtful approach to the subject. In contrast, some groups or individuals sap and drain you, drawing heavily on your emotions. They gain and hold attention by telling their life history, asking continual questions, describing their situation as worse than anyone else's, and hooking onto others in the group.

The danger when you are very tired is of becoming extremely irritated or depressed by individuals and their demands. As trainer, you will want to be sensitive to individuals yet also to give time to others in the group. Otherwise some participants could reasonably feel excluded, as if they're not receiving their money's worth. Furthermore, if you give all your input to one person, you may not have enough to share round. Wherever you train you need to make a clear distinction between the person who has a genuine grievance or complaint which relates to the training and the one for whom work is a continual moan. You listen to the first and try to help them forward. You acknowledge the second and help them back on track.

Amazingly, you can find a professional energy to deal with these trying situations. It may require extra effort to concentrate but it pays off.

The dip in the day

Most people experience a dip in the day, particularly after lunch. You have to work hard to retain the group's interest and keep them awake. You too are not immune to this. Your concentration can go, and your energy level drops. At such times, you may lose confidence or feel that things are not going as well as they could. You may forget for a moment that everything has been fine up until now. It's hard work to keep up the intense concentration required for training. Continuing to project interest and vigour when feeling weary can be tough, so what can you do?

You can do your best to prevent dips in the day by changing the pace of the training and by doing different types of exercises and discussion. However, if the dips do come, first take stock of why this has happened, and then:

- Check whether the others are tired too – the room temperature and atmosphere can affect everyone
- Acknowledge to the participants if your concentration has lapsed: 'Sorry, I missed what you said.'
- Remember how well the training has gone until the 'dip' occurred.
- If possible, give the group something to do so that you can take a back seat for a while for a breather or for thinking time.
- Bring back and harness the energy.
- Relax for a moment and then make a big effort – the adrenalin will get you through.
- Remember that it's not unusual to feel this way – you are not alone.

When the end is in sight with an hour to go, inject extra energy to lift everyone, yourself included. End on a positive note. Though you feel weary inside, you are likely, if you do this, to project a very different picture – that of the calm and confident trainer.

The boredom factor

You're running the same training programme for the umpteenth time or repeating it to several groups. When you're feeling weary, have you ever had the thought, 'I can't face this again'? How do you keep your interest up when the content has become overfamiliar to you? Just remember that it's new and absorbing for the participants. Tap into and enjoy their enthusiasm and interest. Try out new activities and change the way you do the course without losing the content and objectives. This is the challenge which will interest or enthuse you again.

If you have genuinely lost interest don't do it – your participants will know if you're bored.

I've said it before and I'll say it again

> It's Wednesday afternoon and my third group this week. I'm illustrating a point with a favourite story. It always goes down well. They're all looking at me. I've heard myself saying this before – was it today or Monday? I'm not sure.

This sense of déjà vu is likely to happen when you are seeing many different people and repeating the same course in a short space of time. The only thing to do is to check with the group. Ask, 'Have I told you this before?' Usually you haven't. But it's better to take the initiative and let them stop you if necessary, rather than risk boring them.

Pacing yourself

Feast or famine

If you work as a freelancer, this will be familiar fare. You say to yourself, 'I'm definitely going to plan this year, and take breaks when I want to.' Suddenly you are offered some work that you cannot resist, a job that really appeals. All your plans go awry.

> I always look forward to the feast – I feel wanted and successful. But in reality, it's tough. For instance, as a freelancer working for several clients, I find that each one thinks their training is the most important. Of course it is, but what they don't see is that theirs isn't the only work I'm doing. Nor do they see me juggling things. I can't wait for the time when I can be on top of it all again.

Suddenly, there is a famine. The phone goes quiet. There is very little in the diary for the future and you think it's the end of your freelance life. You start to worry about money, and begin to feel depressed. Keeping faith in yourself at these times is hard, but the longer you work freelance, the more you realize that this is the way the work goes. Note whether there is a pattern in the way you work – some months are always quiet.

If you are tired you could use your famine time to good effect. Allow yourself a rest before rushing out to look for more work. Other things to do are:

- Organize some supervision or training for yourself.
- Meet other trainers to discuss developments.
- Update your CV, publicity and training materials.
- Phone the prospective clients you have always been meaning to contact and let them know what you offer.
- Do some of the things you've been putting off for ages.
- Spend the money which you won't have time to spend once you are busy again.

Above all, keep faith and don't lose your confidence as a trainer. Achieving the right balance of training, planning and administrative time can be difficult for the in-house trainer too.

Back-to-back training

The feast can be exhilarating:

> I have difficulties when training is patchy. When I'm at full stretch, I'm at my most energetic. I want to go out after training – I'm on a high. Then I think, 'Oh, for a day in the office'. Yet when I'm there, I don't do the things I'd planned to do.

On the other hand, particularly as an in-house trainer, it can become relentless:

> I certainly don't advise training non-stop, but as I'm involved with so many courses here, it happens. People don't always understand that there's more to the training officer's job than standing up in front of a group of people; it takes considerable thought and preparation time too.

You have to find a balance which suits you and your participants. Back-to-back training can be very tiring. Many trainers realize that they are just going through the motions, missing points, cutting corners and losing their creativity. Even if you are doing off-the-shelf training, you still need time to reconsider the material every now and again, to freshen it up and recharge your batteries, both for your own sake and for the participants'.

Paper mountains

Recognize this scene?

> You're preparing your notes for tomorrow. A pile of handouts from last week's training needs sorting and putting away; you have a list of people

to write to; you need to order stationery, send invoices. Someone rings and asks if you could send your programme – their training brochure goes to the printer next week. You've a report to write on the training which you've just completed.

Some of you will have administrative help, but there still is an enormous amount of paperwork to wade through. It is easy to see this chore as a side-line to training when it is in fact an integral part of the work. Paper work can be oppressive. Much time is spent worrying about it, but people often shy away from tackling it. On the other hand, dealing with paperwork can become a good excuse for not doing the creative work such as planning. One way or another, it saps your energy and can hinder your progress.

Therefore, however you view it, the more organized you are about it the better. Time and money spent on building administrative systems that work will prove an invaluable investment. Being able to lay your hands on the right papers and materials quickly and easily takes away much of the stress. Recognize that you never reach the end of your list – lists are for putting things on as well as for ticking them off.

GUIDELINES

- Do the job straight away or set a deadline for doing it.
- If you aren't going to use the paper, throw it away or pass it on to someone else.
- Ask a good administrator to organize your office for you.
- Organize and classify your handouts; cross reference if necessary.
- Reference handouts and file in subjects.
- Leave handouts behind if you are not going to use them again.
- If you train in time management, try out what you suggest to others – see if it works for you.
- Break down the tasks on your list so that they are possible to do. Also, doing a little from time to time helps you to feel that you are moving on.
- If there is not much training to do, spend time making administration systems that work for you.

Friends in need

Can I have your phone number?

I was caught off guard when the needy victim in the group glided quietly across to me and whispered, 'Can I have your phone number?' Knowing it was the last thing I wanted to do, I found myself giving her my card and hoping that she'd lose it.

GUIDELINES

- Don't allow yourself to be seduced by your own desire not to disappoint, especially if your skills are in enabling vulnerable people – you can't save the entire world.
- Don't make a practice of giving out your personal phone number, though occasionally you may actively choose to do so.
- Pre-empt requests by saying that at the end of the course you'll give contact numbers, and then give a relevant list of numbers you choose to provide, which may or may not include your own.
- Make light of a serious point: tell people you don't make a habit of giving free advice on the phone.
- If someone wants to keep in touch and you would rather not supply your number, ask for theirs and call them.
- If you arrange for someone to call you, or for you to call them, agree in advance the purpose of the call.
- Be clear about what you will and won't do, and stick with it.

Will you be my friend?

I bumped into a participant I'd found very pleasant, and who chanced to live nearby. She was very keen to be friends. I was naïve enough to think she wanted to know me the person, not me the trainer. The first time we met she poured out her troubles, barely stopping for breath, save to ask my advice. I gave her the benefit of the doubt and we met again. The same thing happened again, and again. Each occasion was an exhausting experience, and I felt taken for granted: but once the nature of the relationship had changed from participant/trainer to friend/friend I found it hard to extricate myself.

GUIDELINES

- It helps simply to be aware that when someone says, 'I want to be your friend', it could be a euphemism for 'I'm looking for someone to lean on, and for free!'
- You may decide to set for yourself a strict rule not to develop friendships with participants outside the training context.
- If, however, someone seeks to know you and you feel that you would very much like to know them, also, proceed with caution.

- When you first meet outside training, find out what you have in common apart from training issues.
- This will enable you to appreciate whether they want a true friendship of giving and receiving, or whether they simply want to develop a dependence on you.
- You could set a ground rule before you meet, just as you set ground rules for training. For example, you could say that you would like to see them again, but that you make a clear distinction between your professional and personal life so that you can relax properly when you're not training, and you would therefore appreciate their agreement to avoid the issues you deal with as a trainer.
- If they do start to tell you their troubles, treat it as a warning bell. Remind them of the agreed ground rules, but if these are still not heeded, recognize that this is not about friendship, but a wish to have you there as a free sounding board and adviser.
- It would, however, be a pity to close your mind altogether or be suspicious on every occasion. You might build a warm, enriching and enduring friendship.

A call for help

I find it hard to refuse friends who, knowing what I do, ask me for one-to-one help, either free or for a fee. I worry that I'll appear mean if I refuse, precisely because I do have the professional skills they need, and they have chosen to trust me. The trouble is that it means I can't switch off entirely in my free time. The more tired I am, the harder I find it to refuse.

GUIDELINES

- Weigh up the pros and cons of working with them professionally. Against this course of action is the way it could alter your relationship, and you could end up cutting yourself off from one of your own sources of support. Also, if the problem concerns other people, you may already know them. In favour is that you may enable your friends more quickly than someone else to start off on the right road.
- You can refuse on the basis that you value the friendship, and refer them to someone else for counselling.
- Or you can limit the help you offer by agreeing to see them once or twice only on an advisory basis.
- Be sure that you are effective in maintaining the required boundaries thereafter.

Note that having someone you know on one of your training courses may work perfectly well, always provided that you are not training interpersonal relations to your spouse, or to someone else with whom there could be emotive issues or other unfinished business between you. Once the training group has come to an end, so has your professional relationship with that person. However, in one-to-one requests for help or continued help, the personal/professional boundaries become more clouded.

Watch out for burn-out

All of us become tired, but bounce back after a short rest. Burn-out is different. This happens when you have been working for a long time or for continuous stretches with few breaks. You start to feel tired all the time, demotivated and disinterested. Your creativity and enthusiasm go, and you may lose confidence in your ability to train. In a word, you are stale. It is important to recognize the symptoms. Even if you don't recognize them in yourself – and you don't always – others will. We believe that they are signals to stop.

Trainers who have felt burnt out say that you must take a step back and give yourself time away from training, even if that goes against the grain. You need time to rebuild your physical and emotional reserves, and this may take longer than you think – from a few days to a few months.

To prevent burn-out, pace yourself throughout the year, balancing the busy periods with planned breaks. It is only when you yourself are truly refreshed, that you will be able to refresh others. And that is an essential part of your role as a trainer.

Taking care of yourself

Here are some thoughts on taking care of yourself. They may seem obvious, – but how many of us do the obvious? As trainers, you could become so involved in helping others develop and take care of themselves, that you might forget to heed your own simple advice.

We recognize the difficulties associated with self-discipline, but most trainers agree that it is important to abide by the following ground rules.

Keep fit and healthy

- Have a nutritious diet, avoiding too much tea and coffee.
- Take regular exercise.
- Learn to relax. If you find this hard you might try yoga, t'ai chi, or the Alexander technique.

Look after yourself emotionally

- See a supervisor or counsellor.
- Attend a regular support group.
- Undertake training for yourself.

Take control of your time

- Enter training days on a wall planner so that you can see the pattern.
- Say 'no' to back-to-back training if it feels too much.
- If you don't want to do full-day blocks, or if it will help you and your participants to work more effectively, offer half-day sessions.
- Plan your preparation, administration, course design and handouts well in advance in order to avoid last-minute crises.

Enjoy leisure

- Mark regular holidays and breaks in advance on your planner – then take them.
- If you work at home, don't go to your desk when you're having a break.
- Pursue your interests and hobbies.
- Enter time for family and friends in your diary and keep your appointments with them.

Secure the future

- Arrange financial security through insurance, investment and pension.
- Achieve your personal objectives by career planning.

7 Piggy-in-the-middle

*You can never account for human nature. They tell you one thing, and
do another.*

We call it the 'Piggy-in-the-middle' syndrome. You may not realize that you
are piggy in the middle until you are well into the session – it can happen
unexpectedly. As an independent trainer, you may only learn the true nature
of the group dynamic or the organizational politics as you go along. As an
in-house trainer you have the advantage of knowing the organization well,
but you can also find yourself caught in crossfire or internal politics.

In this chapter, we examine some situations in which trainers may find
themselves, exploring first the difficulties that can occur when the relationship between you and the manager is not clear or when participants view
the manager with suspicion or dislike. Next, since we see change as an
integral part of training, we offer some ideas that may help when you
meet resistance to change. We then consider the danger that arises when
unrealistic expectations are invested in the trainer's ability to resolve an
organization's problems, before going on finally to describe trainers' experiences when they are drawn, perhaps unwittingly, into organizational
politics.

Sometimes you learn a hard lesson and store it away for the next time.
Sometimes you just have to make the best of a difficult situation. At other
times, you can use your piggy-in-the-middle persona to great advantage.
You allow people to bring up difficult issues and express their point of
view. You help groups use conflict positively to find solutions. You can
mediate or negotiate. You can bring people together by asking the questions
that 'no one has dared to ask before'.

Although being in the middle can be a strong and a powerful position,
it can also cause dilemmas. There may be times when, because information
has been kept back, or because you have only been given one side of the
story, you are not sure precisely what is going on. You gather information

as you proceed and begin to piece it together. On occasion, you realize during the training that all is not as it seems or that something is amiss.

Points may come up that worry you. What if you discover that there is bad practice going on? Who do you tell? When do you breach a contract of confidentiality? When does your role change from trainer to mediator, or even counsellor? These dilemmas arise even for the most experienced trainer. As an involved trainer you will be sensitive to people's needs and feelings. You will have to make decisions about how far you go.

Management matters

Obviously it helps to clarify both your position and people's attitude to the training before you start. But you cannot always do this, and you may be caught out when you discover that the division of responsibilities between trainer and manager and your respective roles in the project are unclear. For instance, a manager in a group may find it hard to accept that in this setting you are the leader. Conversely, he or she may want you to take responsibility for difficulties which are patently his or hers to deal with.

Even experienced managers may initially feel vulnerable in front of you. They may see the training as an implicit criticism. It could appear that they have been unable to resolve the problem themselves or have not done their job properly, so you have been called in. You need to be sensitive to these very natural feelings.

The manager in the group

You can find yourself as piggy when a manager feels uncomfortable in the group or refuses any discussion with you beforehand, asserting that there are no problems and that the staff can say what they like. It is only once the training is underway that they may realize the implications of this. Either the group says very little or they bring out all sorts of resentments. Your responsibility is to create a safe place in which to discuss difficult issues, but you will also need to maintain the manager's 'role'. This could mean challenging the manager and the participants.

A well-managed team is a big advantage for the trainer and having the manager in the group can be extremely positive. If you have discussed his or her role beforehand and clarified the role during the training, this will avoid either of you being caught in the middle.

The manager may choose to relinquish the 'role' during the session, or to remain in it and respond from that position. You and the participants, including the manager, need to understand what happens to any group decisions in terms of:

- what will happen afterwards, and how the group will follow up the decisions;
- where the manager's responsibilities begin and end; and
- how much power she or he has to act on any issues raised in the training.

You need clear agreements on the points so that there is no retribution for the group or flak for the manager at a later stage. Staff have responsibilities too: honesty and openness does not mean a forum for the group to gang up on or bash the manager.

'It's the management'

> We were working well. People were being honest about what they thought needed looking at, when someone, asked to suggest the way forward, said, 'It's up to the management'. The others nodded, glad to lay the responsibility for doing things on someone else. In this instance 'management' was actually sitting in the room – she was the sole manager. The shock on her face was visible and it took her a little time to recognise that although they related well to her on a personal level, they also wanted to saddle her with all the ills and difficulties of the organization.

The trainer could not have prepared for what happened here, although the manager's prior understanding of her role during the training and her 'permission' for openness helped. Thus, having set up a clear framework with the group and the manager, the trainer could challenge the group without taking sides:

> I said, 'But the management's here – it's not a thing, she's with you'. I didn't want to humiliate the manager by rescuing her. I didn't want to take sides, but I did feel for her. I needed to make the group think about where their responsibilities lay and what 'management' means. How much can they 'manage' themselves?

GUIDELINES

- Support the manager's 'role', but also allow others to bring up difficult issues. Do this by setting a clear working framework and agreeing the ground rules with the group and manager.

- You have taken on the leader's role in the training. Use it to encourage two-sided views and to avoid negative 'them' and 'us' dialogues.
- Encourage managers to clarify their position in the training session at the beginning, with a statement such as: 'During this training period I am part of the group. I am not participating as your manager.' This gives the group permission to talk openly. But you need to offer your support to managers, because they may well be subjected to critical comments.
- Managers who are happy to relinquish their position during training are usually confident in their role and open to discussion. You can help them by bringing an objectivity to the proceedings, and by raising sensitive issues within a clear framework.
- Good working relationships within groups are usually the result of good management. Managers are not always aware of how this contributes to the training, or are modest about it. Give them the credit by telling them, 'It's a real tribute to you'.

Do you tend to empathize with those you are currently working with? When you work with managers you see things from their point of view. Then you work with others in the organization and you do the same with them.

The monster in manager's clothing

'If the manager went, it would all be different. We hate the boss,' they cried with one voice. 'He's rude, critical and never has time for us. He thinks praise is a four-letter word.' I began to picture this ogre. I was feeling sorry for the group and wanting to see him on their behalf. No wonder they were all feeling devalued and demotivated.

Soon after, I met this monster in manager's clothing. Was this really the person they were so incensed with? I was left with the impression of an intelligent, thoughtful individual, who no doubt set high standards for his staff but who also had their interests at heart, though he did say he could be moody in times of stress.

I wondered why there was such an 'us' and 'them' attitude on the part of the staff, where the communication had broken down. It was a real lesson to me on how easy it is to be drawn in, and so curry favour with the underdog.

GUIDELINES

- Listen empathetically to complaints about appraisals, restructuring and downsizing and about the bully disguised as manager, but look also for people's personal power so that they can find their own solutions for dealing with the problem.

- Ask people to concentrate on specific issues – steer them away from the global complaint about the organization. Encourage them to take responsibility for at least one thing, however small, which they can do to change their own situation or way of working.
- Remember you are hearing only one side, so be careful not to make judgements. If you are not part of the organization, it may take some time before you find out the real truth about relationships among staff. It is not always as it seems. As an in-house trainer, you may agree with the participants and can give appropriate feedback to the organization, but you also need to provide participants with their own strategies for dealing with the situation – you are not there simply to rescue them.
- Analyse carefully how the culture of the organization affects communication between individuals. For example, a very hierarchical organization may stop people expressing what they want. Conversely, working in a co-operative could inhibit people from disagreeing with each other.
- Counter some of the established behaviour patterns by using practical exercises and activities that give people permission and safety to speak out. Learning to communicate differently may not suddenly change the culture, but it can start people thinking.
- Allow participants to express negative emotions as a means of release but not as an end in itself.
- Don't take sides against anyone – the workers, the boss, the organization. Your most positive asset from everyone's point of view is that you can see both sides, that you have an objectivity which can cut through some of the old patterns of relationships.
- You can act as go-between or catalyst for people who find it hard to communicate with each other. You can encourage them to discuss the issues together and look at ways of solving problems.

The manager and you

Several trainers described 'manager problems' of a rather different nature, that is, not between participants and manager, but between trainer and manager. This is particularly awkward for in-house trainers, but not exclusive to them. The following tale represents the tip of the iceberg.

Standing in the shadows

My boss is always standing in the shadows or looking directly over my shoulder. Some days he hovers outside the door; on others he bursts in and takes over the group. I can be right in the middle of a sentence. I feel inhibited and undermined. I'm worried that I'll totally lose confidence if I don't put a stop to this behaviour once and for all. How on earth can I keep my integrity as well as a good relationship with my manager?

In discussing this situation we agreed how hard it is to concentrate and do good work with anyone breathing down your neck, let alone your manager. The problem is you don't know that this is going to happen – it just does, and then you're stuck with it. And, it's much harder to undo what has been done than to prevent it in the first place.

In the event of intrusion or someone trying to take over your show, therefore, there is no alternative to a polite, honest but direct approach. Tell them that you feel disconcerted when they come in and watch or take over, and that while you are pleased by their interest, nevertheless you will be more effective as a trainer if you work with clear responsibilities. Agree your roles so that you maintain your authority as a trainer.

Managing change

Coping with change has little to do with known routines, safety and familiarity. Yet it is an essential part of any developing organization, and as trainer you have a key role in helping people manage it. You raise people's awareness so that they recognize when they need to change, and you suggest strategies and introduce skills that help them do this.

You may understand the difficulties and recognize the fears that surround change and create resistance, but dealing with constant resistance to change can sap your confidence or make you feel like giving up. Convincing participants that change can bring positive development is a hard task when they are genuinely distressed or when they find it easier to stay where they are and blame others.

If training is seen as the sole answer to managing change, then there is a danger that you will become the piggy in the middle. Your role and what you can realistically offer have to be clear. It is the manager's role to make the change happen and see it through with the staff. You are there to help them manage the change, not to change the organization. Certainly the organization may change as a result of your one day's training, but that's too high an expectation in most circumstances and will only leave you and the participants frustrated and angry.

New systems and structures

There has just been another reorganization. The participants arrive feeling disgruntled and so taken up with what is going on around them that it is difficult for them to concentrate on the training. What you offer them seems irrelevant in the face of so much upheaval in their day-to-day work. They see no point in learning new skills.

A trainer describes here a situation in which he used to best advantage his piggy-in-the-middle position once he realized what was happening in the organization.

> I was running a customer care course as part of a drive to improve customer care ratings in the face of insufficient staff, deteriorating product quality and a severe backlog of letters and phone calls. The participants were glum and unresponsive. By lunchtime, I felt as if I had been pushing water uphill all morning.
>
> At lunchtime, the manager and her assistant breezed in, announced a reorganization that they had decided would solve the backlog, and breezed out again. I didn't think it was possible, but the atmosphere deteriorated even further.
>
> For the first time I asked them what was wrong, sharing with them my concerns about their lack of response. They immediately poured out their feelings about the way they were managed and their belief (which I shared, having heard their story) that customer care training would make no difference.

The trainer described how he took a risk:

> I decided there and then to abandon the course, and offered to help them in their relationship with their boss.

He used his position as piggy in the middle to bring matters to a head. He didn't take away the participants' responsibility to do something themselves about the situation, but he:

- helped them to devise a framework for how they would like to be managed and coached them in how they would put this to their boss;
- helped them determine what they would have to do in return for being more empowered;
- role-played their request for a meeting with their boss the same day; and
- gave them the skills to negotiate.

His risk paid off:

> A meeting was arranged for later that afternoon. Apparently it went on until early evening. I telephoned the boss the next morning expecting to be told not to darken their door again. Her response couldn't have been more different. The meeting had been a great success, many issues had been resolved, and she was pleasantly surprised at the motivation of her staff.

The trainer concluded:

> I learned from this episode not to take what the manager might tell me before the course at face value, but to probe more deeply. I also learned not to be afraid to respond to the needs of the participants if that meant shifting from the original brief.

What's the point?

'We've tried that, but it doesn't work' or 'There's nothing we can do'. It is hard to remain enthusiastic and optimistic in the face of such complaint. Yet these are the moments when you have to call on all your reserves to avoid a complete meltdown of the group. You meet groups that feel powerless to express their anger directly to the management and who throw their frustrations at you. And there are also the cynical or disillusioned, who, finding that working life is not as easy as it used to be, hope that you won't put any more pressure on them.

> They had been in the organization for a long time. Now they were subject to increasing expectations and calls for more accountability. They resented this, feeling powerless as the lowest-paid group. They greeted every new idea with 'They'll never listen'. I was becoming very frustrated. 'Aren't you represented on the management committee?', I asked. 'They don't want us,' the most vociferous replied. 'But you could go on, couldn't you?', I insisted. 'Who would be prepared to go on the committee?' No one spoke and I probed again. There was shoulder shrugging and a quiet 'It's no use'. But I felt that I had stopped the rot, and the moaning stopped too for a while.
> I accept that people have to be allowed to let off steam, but you need to show them reality too, to help them to put their energy into something they can or want to do something about.

As participants pour out their gripes and unhappiness, you can easily find yourself being drawn into the protesting culture. However, it's one thing to give the group gripe water, to allow them to purge the bad feelings out of their system before they move on. It's quite another to openly sympathize with what, after all, is only one side of the argument, and possibly an illusion on their part. You are colluding with the blaming culture and implying, 'Yes, I agree with you. It's their fault. And there's nothing we can do to make things better.'

Groups like the one in the tale above can irritate or frustrate you. Use your irritation as a barometer – it usually indicates that you need to move on. Bring participants back on track after the initial moaning. Focus on what it is possible for them to do and help them to express these opinions.

Working miracles

The quick fix

'We'd like you to do stress management in half a day,' they tell me. I feel caught between their objectives and budget on the one hand and what I deem to be in the best interests both of the participants and the organization on the other.

Many trainers complain that they are being asked to telescope material into shorter and shorter periods. Plain economics combined with a reluctance to allow staff away from their desks at times of pressure create the perceived need for a quick fix, but that is a false economy. Sometimes it simply reflects a lack of regard for the value of training. So how can you gain back control and feel less of a piggy?

GUIDELINES

- Clarify precisely what you can and cannot do. Whatever you finally put into the course, you have to convey to the client and participants both the benefits and limitations of the session. If you don't convey the benefits, they will question whether it is worthwhile; if you don't present the limitations, they will feel shortchanged. At the outset, when you describe the outline and objectives, state what they can realistically expect, and what further training could fulfil their wider expectations.
- Tell participants that this is just a taster.
- Be aware of participants who feel caught between wanting a longer course and worrying about how they'll cope with the backlog of their work. You do not want to cause further stress on stress management courses.

- Try to negotiate a longer course with the client. Underline the benefits of running one- or two-day courses.
- If you are not happy doing the course in half a day, don't do it.
- Negotiate the content of a shortened course. Point out the advantages of participants covering a few topics fully rather than skimming the surface of many.
- If they insist on, say, twenty topics, clarify what you and the participants can expect to achieve. Explain that you will probably need to use fast-moving techniques like brainstorming, or input by you which will not allow much participation and deductions by the participants.
- Combine lecturing with mini-practice and time your content in a highly disciplined way. Never start something and then tell the participants that you haven't time to complete it. You know that you have had to make choices and miss out some of your favourite exercises or ways of doing things – they will never know.
- Confirm in writing the course objectives, content, style, approach and time limitations. You may want to include a statement such as: 'The trainer reserves the right, within course objectives, to retain flexibility in order to respond to group and individual needs to meet their best interest.' This enables you to make it relevant to the group.
- Adults learn most effectively and feel more empowered when they have opportunities for deducing things themselves, so try to give an opportunity for this somewhere in the programme. The time may be a restriction here.

The last resort

'Let's send her on a training day', meaning, let's see if someone else can make her toe the line. There is complete misunderstanding about what training offers. The person sent may be resentful, while the managers may be either at the end of their tether with that person, or expecting too much of the training. You may successfully involve the person during the training – indeed, you may help the person to be more aware – but how far can you as the trainer influence things?

> 'See what you can do – we've practically reached the end of the road with him.' They knew that he wasn't up to the job, but that they would have difficulty in dismissing him. So they were sending him on training, partly, I suspected, to get him out of the office. I find this a dilemma. In fact, I think the person benefited from the training personally, but it did not solve his work situation. I can do something about training, but nothing about his performance afterwards.

GUIDELINES

- Avoid adopting the position of judge or jury. It is easy to be drawn in, particularly as an in-house trainer, and especially if the participant has a reputation within the organization. As an external trainer, don't be swayed in your judgement by hearsay. Keep an open mind and concentrate on the content and process of the course, while taking into account the person's difficulties.
- Recognize your position here. Be clear about confidentiality and don't take sides. If both manager and participant are complaining to you, concentrate on what each can do about it.
- Be clear from the start what the training offers. It can give skills and strategies and you can help the participant to understand how they can use these, but the manager needs to follow up the training in the workplace.
- Ask the participant whether or not she or he chose to come to the training, and what she or he feels about this situation.
- Talk to the manager and participant about how they can follow up the training and help the person's performance. Identify some steps which they could take together or individually.
- Feed back to the manager only with the permission of the participant. You could do this via flipchart notes or you might arrange a meeting for the three of you to discuss what happens next.
- Use your piggy-in-the-middle position positively. You can advise both sides or mediate if necessary.

People and politics

Trainers are frequently on the receiving end of anger about the organization and how it is run. Sometimes, as the trainer below relates, you may have to accept criticism for things which are outside your remit or beyond your control. You become the punchball for people's anger. As a result, you may feel angry too; you may even feel that you have been set up.

Taking the flak

An inspector calls

As in most educational establishments the day came when I was told: 'An inspector will call.' Unannounced she or he would come in for half an hour, sit at the side, write copious notes, sit in silent judgement and go without a word.

I wasn't wild about the idea, and because it was a counselling skills course with an agreement of confidentiality, this complicated matters. I knew some of my group would object, which they did.

In explaining to your group the reasons for this seemingly unwelcome intrusion, it is worth clarifying any negativity you feel about the situation, over which you have little control.

There may well be some benefits too. You could point out that:

- The inspector will observe and feed back to, and about, you (the trainer) not them (the participants).
- It is part of the procedure, and there is nothing you can do to prevent it.
- You feel uncomfortable because of the group's right to privacy and confidentiality, but there is nothing you can do to prevent the visit. They must therefore take responsibility for what they discuss while the Inspector is present. If possible, tell them how long she or he is likely to be there.
- You will see if you can negotiate for the inspector to come at a particular time, though that is not always possible.
- Inspections can only occur during training delivery and it is therefore important to co-operate.
- The inspector could make a valuable contribution to quality assurance, so that the organization offers participants only the best in training.
- The organization might attract more funding as a result of the visit.
- If anyone still isn't happy, they can choose not to contribute during the visit or else withdraw from the room to coincide with the inspector's call.

Camera shy

Halfway through the morning the co-ordinator thrust a note into my hand saying: 'Please tell the group that TV cameras are filming tomorrow.' Presented to me as a fait accompli, I dutifully told them.

Most were thrilled that they would be stars for a day, but one was incensed at 'being spied on' and stormed off. Faced with all manner of threats from this one participant, the organizer repented and decided to forfeit publicity for peace and quiet. 'Please tell the group there won't be any TV cameras tomorrow,' said she, leaving me to do the dirty work.

I had been party to neither decision, yet I presented both to the group. I felt a complete fool and well aware of their annoyance with me, one for giving the news, the rest for retracting it.

There's a moral to this story: let course organizers give, and retract, their own messages. Don't do it for them.

Economical with the truth

Someone is economical with the truth. You are cast as a spy or the enemy. You find yourself in the middle of a dispute which should have been resolved outside the training room.

> There were obvious signs of stress in the group, and we could not understand why they were so suspicious of us. During the course, they did no more than we required and no-one asked questions. At the end, they complained to the department about our attitude as trainers. We found this difficult to comprehend. It was only then that we discovered that on their last course, they had, without being told, been assessed. They thought we were doing the same and wanted to give their view of the training before we did. In fact, after the course, we were asked to submit a report. We refused.

Sometimes, as this trainer relates, you are caught in a situation that you cannot understand until afterwards. But as he relates, he kept his integrity.

GUIDELINES

- When you can speak frankly before the session, ask: Is there anything I need to know which will help or hinder the training?
- Then find out from both sides what they want to achieve from the training.
- When you are doing the training, if you feel that you are making little progress or the group is being evasive, stop the training and ask participants what is going on, whether they want to discuss anything.
- If there is no response, continue with the programme, but check frequently with the participants to see if they have any comments or questions.
- Use the breaks as an informal time to discuss their working experiences.

Reporting back

Throughout this book, we have stressed the importance of confidentiality with participants. Yet reporting back on a course can be important if there is going to be follow-up in the workplace. Obtaining the participants' permission, and trusting that the manager will both act on the feedback and act with integrity, is vital.

The group flatly refused to feed back their ideas to the organization. I felt frustrated because I wanted their ideas to be heard. They hated the changes, and they were worried about losing their jobs. They didn't believe I could do anything for them and as for the manager – there was no point in discussing it with her. I felt awkward talking to the manager. I didn't know her very well and there was not an instant trust or rapport between us. I had told her that I would be making an agreement of confidentiality with the group. She expected some feedback. In the event they did not give me permission to do this. I was definitely the piggy in the middle on this occasion, and I had made no progress with either side.

This is of course an extreme example. The trainer had followed the guidelines below, but you may recognize her dilemma.

GUIDELINES

- Tell the manager that you will be making an agreement of confidentiality with the group and there is the possibility that they will not want to report back. This is not usually the case.
- Make sure that everybody is clear about what confidentiality means. It is acceptable to talk about issues, but you don't reveal people's personal views unless they agree to this.
- Report back through the written flipchart notes so that they come as general comments. Ask people if they want anything removed before the notes go to the manager.
- Never break confidentiality.

Conspiracy

There had been some redundancies and several changes in the organization, but the new manager was committed to regular staff training for all levels. Most of the group had been in their jobs for a long time and had received little or no training. I'm used to working with people new to training and when I'd been arranging the training I had gone round and introduced myself to the people so that they knew who they would be getting. I started off cheerfully, putting people at their ease, or so I thought. They responded, but without much enthusiasm. I put this reaction down to anxiety and explained the framework for working, and asked them what they wanted to gain from the training. They were polite, and set off doing the first exercise. I couldn't put my finger on it, but I knew there was something wrong – they only half trusted me. We had the coffee break. 'Right,' I said, 'so how's the training so far?' A woman offering me coffee became the spokesperson. 'Tell us', she said, 'why are they suddenly making us do all this training. They never took any notice of us before. What's going on?'

It took me quite a long time to convince them that as far as I was concerned I was here to offer training that would be useful to them, and that I had nothing to do with any conspiracy. I realized that although I'd found out about the training needs from the manager, I hadn't done my homework properly on the history of the organization. Or perhaps I would not have discovered much beforehand, anyway.

GUIDELINES

- Before the training, find out what experience the participants have had in the organization.
- Explain to the group why you have come, what you can offer, and what they stand to gain from it.
- Expect participants to take time to trust you, particularly if they see you as being sent in by the management.
- Ask why they think they haven't had training before and what they see as their needs. They may see these aspects differently from the managers.
- If a group is reluctant, find out why. People may feel more comfortable talking about this informally over coffee, rather than as a direct challenge in the group.
- If one or two people tell you how they feel, suggest to them that you talk to the whole group about this, and see if they are in agreement with this suggestion.

Summary

The stories in this chapter are all from experienced trainers who did their homework beforehand.

To do your best to either avoid or cope with being piggy in the middle, remember:

- The more you know before you start, the better. Forewarned is forearmed.
- You can feel foolish or downright angry, coming away with a sense of failure, if you feel that you have been set up.
- There are times when you cannot go further. You can only go as far as others allow you.

- You may have to put the experience behind you, but you may learn something useful too.
- At times, 'piggy in the middle' is a powerful position that opens the way for new thinking, strategies and solutions.

8 Hello and action

You don't look like a trainer.

In this chapter we emphasize the importance of clear beginnings to training sessions, and examine the assumptions both trainers and trainees can make about each other. We then give some ideas to help participants settle in, and discuss how you introduce them to the programme and the way you will be working.

First impressions

The first moments are often the most difficult for participants. The way you welcome them, set the scene and relax them into the session has a profound effect on the rest of training. Here we explore what happens when people arrive, their first impressions and yours, and what you can do and say to make a positive start.

It is said that you only have one chance to make a first impression, and that it takes seven seconds to look someone up and down and pigeonhole them. First impressions can be powerful, though they can change as you learn more about the person – provided you give them the chance.

What we look like to them

Before the course:

> They said there would be someone to meet me at the station. I arrived and waited. Finally, I went up to someone who was obviously waiting and asked if he was looking for me. 'Are you a trainer?' He seemed surprised. 'Yes,' I replied. 'Well, you don't look like one.'

Dress and demeanour are vitally important to a trainer, but what does a trainer look like? Participants often have preconceptions about tall, power dressers waltzing in amid a blaze of confidence. They are expecting you to wear a smart suit with a good cut and a designer label. So when you don't, some will feel put out, others relieved.

On the day

However, if you look completely at variance with the culture of the organization, you might find it hard to establish your authority with the group.
   A training officer explained:

> I was working for a smart city financial firm. I needed a last-minute substitute for a trainer who had gone down with 'flu. From the look of the details supplied by the trainer and talking to her over the phone, she clearly knew her stuff. But I was shocked when she turned up to do the training in a hippy dress and leather-thonged sandals. I knew some of the group would look down their noses at her, and they did. She never had a chance to use her wealth of experience for the benefit of the company.

You have to look the part. It's one thing to dress for comfort, but not exclusively so. You must to some extent reflect or fit in with the culture of the organization. This does not imply that you have to deny your own comfort and identity. Indeed, if you feel or look uncomfortable this will quickly be conveyed to your participants.

> I choose my clothes with immense care. I don't want to look too hard, or too soft. So power dressing is out, so are pink chiffon blouses. As a dark jacket is supposed to lend authority, I opt for it if I feel rather fragile. I wear a lighter one if I think my group might feel vulnerable. I aim for comfort with authority.
>   I like loose fitting clothes so that I'm not restricted. I would hate my jacket to rip as I reached up to write on the flipchart. The more relaxed I am, the more likely they are to relax in my presence.
>   I try not to wear anything that will distract me or them, like spots and stripes, vivid patterns, clanky jewellery or high heels that go clip clop. Some patterns are particularly tiring on the eyes and I must remember that the group will be looking at me for much of the day.

It is not only how you dress that impresses itself on participants as they arrive, but also the way you conduct yourself.

Demeanour

A participant described how he approached someone in the room when he arrived and asked:

> 'Do you know when the trainer's going to come?' 'I am the trainer' was the reply. He explained: 'She gave the impression by the way she sat and looked so casual that she was one of the participants. She lacked the air of authority I need a trainer to have so that I can feel confident in them.'

A trainer who looks much younger than she is explains the effect this can have on a participant and how she deals with it:

> One of the admin staff on the course made a beeline for me in the break. 'You look very young. I said to my mum last night, 'She's just a girl.' People often expect you to be older, and wiser, than they are. So when you're not what they expect, you need to establish your credibility for them to feel confidence in you.'

This trainer does this by telling the group at the outset her training qualifications, how long she's been a trainer and who some of her clients are.

'Ello, 'ello, who have we here?

What they look like to us

Several trainers described how they watched people arriving:

> I watch them come in. The first, in tee-shirt and jeans, greets me in a friendly way. Someone shy hovers near the door, so I bring her in and make her feel at home. Three men come in together, clearly from the same department, all in white shirts and ties, mobile phones attached to their belts. The room gradually fills up. I find myself making judgements all the time – she looks relaxed, he looks tense, will I have trouble with her, is he on the right course, and so on. As I watch them, they are also watching me and sizing me up.

> I look to see who I know, and who I don't. I always go over and greet people I've met before. I wouldn't want to snub them, or have them think I'd forgotten who they are. But I also might think, 'Oh good, she was fun' or 'Oh no, not them again'.

I'm very conscious of the hoverers, those who are clearly nervous and need some encouragement. So I give it. I go over, welcome them and briefly introduce myself. Show them where the coffee is. I do the same if I notice someone looks downcast. But I try not to become too involved when I'm about to begin.

I'm watching for the mix, how old or young, how many men and women, noticing the apparent cross-cultural mix. Most things I won't know until we start talking, like who is the manager, but already I'm thinking about how I might divide up the group for exercises, and how they'll choose to divide up. Where will the alliances form? Who do I have to watch for caucusing that might exclude others?

I know I prejudge. I'm thinking, just by looking at their body language, who will be for me, and who against? Yet I know I can't make assumptions. They might turn out very different.

The things you do

Both you and the group need time to settle in before you start the formal training. In this respect, the environment and resources provided by the organisation and your approach, make a substantial difference. You have arrived early to set up and to deal with any crises. You can then do much to set the tone and make the participants feel wanted.

Before the audience arrives you check that everything is exactly as you would like to find it if you were attending the course. One trainer describes:

I like people to feel special. I make sure there's coffee, both with and without caffeine, tea and herbal teas, and a choice of biscuits. Sometimes I bring cake or chocolates for afternoon tea. I place flowers on a side-table towards the front. If the venue has a patio or garden, I encourage them to have their drinks outside before we start. I make sure the room has been warmed up or cooled down, depending on the time of year, and that I have access to a fan, air conditioning or heating. If people's practical needs are met, they can concentrate on the job of learning.

Welcome everyone as they arrive with a 'Hello', a smile and a brief introduction. Invite them to take refreshments and indicate where to have coffee and where the training takes place. If there is a sudden rush of people coming in, at least nod and smile to each one. This means you are fully prepared before they arrive. The last thing that you want to be doing at that stage is sitting at your desk, head down, scribbling, or standing with your back to them while you prepare a flipchart.

Leaving a course programme on their seats with a sticky label for their names gives them something useful to do rather than sitting in awkward silence. You might open a few minutes later than the official start time on the first day. However, beginning when you said you would sets an organized tone for the rest of the course and respects those who have arrived early.

The things you say

Invite everyone to take a seat and welcome them, briefly introducing yourself and what the course is about. This is that critical point in the training where you set a safe learning environment. They need to know who you are, who else is there, what the facilities are, what the ground rules are, where you are taking them, and how they will be expected to participate. In preparing to prepare them, you need to step into their shoes and think about what you would need to feel at your ease if you were the participant.

> I welcome them as a group, but I try to catch the eye of each person there. I thank them for coming and say how pleased I am to meet them. To bring them together quickly, I start with what unites them. Stating the common ground helps link individuals from the outset.
>
> I make a group contract. I write it on the flipchart, agree it with them and display it throughout the course. If someone breaches it, I can refer back to it. It's a way of unifying them around an agreement, and we all know where we stand. I see it as fundamental to a safe learning environment.
>
> I tell the group that different people have different ways of dealing with situations: for example, some will talk a lot and some not at all. In counselling and personal growth I also say that what anyone is feeling is legitimate, and if you want to cry, that's fine. I'm normalising behaviour. A ground rule about both listening carefully and not talking too long helps everyone manage this.

Summary

- Write to participants before the course inviting them to come 15 to 30 minutes before your formal beginning to have refreshments and meet other people.
- Dress both for comfort and for the organization and participants.
- Have refreshments and other special touches at the ready.
- Greet each person individually.

- Invite them to take drinks and eats.
- Ask them to sit down when you're ready.
- Welcome them as a group.
- Introduce yourself, establishing your credibility with your qualifications, experience, clients or other relevant information.
- Say how you came to be training if it has relevance to the course.
- Do the domestics, like fire regulations, break and lunch times, where the toilets are.
- Ask what special requirements there are, like needing to sit near the flipchart or the trainer, to see or to hear.
- Go through the course outline and how you expect them to participate, while offering an element of choice.
- Allow time for questions.
- Tell them to ask if at any time they can't read, hear or understand something or in some way need help.

Now they're sitting comfortably, you can begin.

9 The reluctant trainee

In one day, I have to get through the dross, get them interested, transform the world and make sure they get the 4.30 bus.

In this chapter we introduce people who come to training with a heavy heart or without enthusiasm. We call them reluctant trainees. You will probably recognize some of them, but, as in the rest of the book, although based on real situations, the details have been changed.

Beginning at the beginning, we find out why people are on the course and how they feel about it, and we suggest some ways of easing the tensions. There will be some who have never been on a course or experienced your kind of training before, and we examine their situation. We then describe a range of behaviours which you meet during the sessions, from the sleepy to the refusers, and how you might respond to them, before considering finally some ways of ensuring that people participate and become involved.

Reluctance to training is expressed in many ways: passivity, belligerence, refusal or fear of participating, choosing to be late or finding constant distractions. The reasons are diverse; the participants are apprehensive if they are new to training or had a previous bad experience, bored if they feel they have had a surfeit. Training may be an easy option, a day out or a chance to vent all the pent up feelings they have been storing up about the organization. Some assume that it will be a 'wasted day' – work at the desk is much more important. As trainer you are aware that you need to put on hold your external worries and concerns and concentrate hard on the job. Some participants may not see it this way.

One trainer categorizes trainees as: participants, passengers, protesters and prisoners. The participants are involved; they accept you and your role, and have much to offer in the learning process. You are always pleased to have them there. The passengers come along for the ride – for them, it's just a couple of days out of the office. They don't offer much but then they don't cause much trouble either. Their expectations are limited to the hope that you will let them out early, that the lunch will be worth having, and that they won't be asked to do too much. The protester we consider in the next chapter about the troublesome trainee.

The prisoner has been sent by the boss. She or he may be feeling inadequate or very angry, and would much rather be somewhere else but believes there is no choice. You often have sympathy for the prisoner and you may be able to release him or her, but sometimes you may be cast as the warder.

In the event, many who start off as reluctant trainees eventually relax, become involved and offer a tremendous amount once they know that you recognize and understand their reluctance. Others will prove more difficult to interest or change.

Arrivals

Did you jump or were you sent?

Knowing in advance whether people have been sent or chose to come gives you a head start in building up a relationship with them, although the information is not always available beforehand.

The 'prisoner'

> Quite obviously he hadn't opted for the training.
> 'So what would you rather be doing?' I asked.
> 'I'd rather be at the pictures.'
> 'So why don't you go?' I said, and told him what was showing at the local cinema. We suddenly had something in common, talking about films. I had also given him a choice. He decided to stay. He was fine after that.

You often spot the 'prisoner' by the body language – sitting outside the group, nursing the 'I'm not going to enjoy this' look.

If the manager has been straightforward in requesting the person to attend, the participant may be angry, but you will at least be able to discuss this with him or her. If, on the other hand, there have been heavy hints or the manager has made an offer that is difficult to refuse – for example, a promotion depends on attendance or it is part of disciplinary action – then you can find yourself with a very resentful or distressed person. Whatever the circumstances, always acknowledge the participant's feelings.

Furious from Finance

Have you ever been faced by the following at the beginning of a session?

> I only heard last night that this was happening today. I've got a desk full of work and I don't see why I need to come. This training has no relevance to what I do.

GUIDELINES

- Acknowledge that people may not want to be with you and ask at the outset who has been sent. You can lighten the question by asking, 'Did you jump or were you pushed?'
- Allow people to express their feelings. They are likely to vent their anger on you, but you need to avoid the 'them and us' relationship where they see you in the other camp and begin to blame you for their predicament. If you don't, you may find yourself as the 'piggy in the middle' (see Chapter 7). Ask how the participant feels about attending: 'How do you feel about being here?' 'Why do you feel like this?' 'What are you worried about?' 'How could you benefit from the training?'
- You are starting afresh with participants. Make a distinction between the role of manager and trainer. You are not the manager and you may be able to give them some choice. If not, you can show that you recognize that the person has to attend.
- Reassure them that the training is *for them* and try to draw them in, using their experience.
- You may be able to give some power back by giving them choice within the training and saying: 'I understand you don't think it's relevant, but take what you can. It has wide application and you just might find something relevant to you.'
- Ask, 'How do you think you can make it relevant to you?'
- Participants may have more choice than they think. You could suggest that they go back and discuss it with the manager. Or you might propose: 'Stay till the break and see what you think, whether your feelings have changed. Then decide.'
- When you give people choice they may leave, but don't take this as a negative reflection on yourself. Once they know that you understand how they are feeling, the chances are that they will stay and participate. They often give the most positive evaluation at the end, too.

First timers

New to training

They have worked in the organization for a long time – perhaps as manual workers, support staff, auxiliaries, volunteers. The last time they attended a 'class' was at school, and their previous experience of learning may not have been particularly rewarding. People don't usually ask their opinion at work, but they have a wealth of experience.

If this is the first time they have been offered training, they may be wary: 'They've never offered training before – why now?' There is a suggestion of conspiracy here. Or they are very excited – this is the beginning of something new. Their expectations could be very low or very high. There is anxiety. People worry that they will look foolish, not know the answer, not understand, or be singled out. They may not usually attend meetings and are frightened of speaking up in a group. Training language and conventions are new to them. You are the 'expert', so they expect that you will probably give a lecture and a boring one at that.

The opening can determine how the rest of the course will go. You want the participants to see the training as worthwhile, enjoyable and for their benefit.

GUIDELINES

- Make no assumptions. There is a 'freshness' about people new to training. They will often say exactly what they think. They won't use the jargon, so make sure you don't.
- Set out clearly at the beginning what the course is about, even if they have had a programme. Explain what your role is, how you are going to give input, how they will be involved, and the importance of their contributions.
- Ask them what they are expecting and what their worries are about attending a course. Some may be angry about being sent on a course, others thrilled at the opportunity of some training at last.
- People often find it strange when you set out the ground rules, but these are very important. Explain that the rules are 'a way of working together' and check that they understand them and agree. You may want to add an additional comment like, 'You're allowed to be nervous', and you will certainly want to emphasize the importance of differences and how we can use them positively. Avoid appearing to lay down the rules – they are agreements. You are setting up a safe place. You want to avoid being cast as the 'teacher', and you must clarify

your role as the 'facilitator' who makes sure that things happen and that people are heard.

- Saying to people, 'Ask questions if you don't understand', does not necessarily work. People feel awkward asking, so you need to check constantly that they understand. People are often worried when asked to do exercises, and so don't hear the instructions. Make sure that people are clear about what is happening.
- Some participants will find it impossible to speak in a large group. Make sure, therefore, that there are plenty of group activities. Move them round, so that the same people don't stick together all the time.
- People unused to training may find it hard to sustain focused discussions. Keep the discussions short and set down some leading questions for them. Sometimes stop the group and ask: 'How many of you are still on track?' This usually raises a laugh as people realize they have wandered off the point. It also helps to stop the lengthy anecdote and gives others an opportunity to make a contribution.
- Explain what you mean by anecdotes, so that people do not spend their time telling personal stories which may be boring to others and irrelevant.
- Training terms (e.g. 'feedback', 'brainstorm', 'ground rules') are often new to people. Explain what you mean if you use such terms.
- Check on literacy levels beforehand. Asking people to write feedback on large sheets or to read out information could be embarrassing for them. If you ask people to write things up, assure them that there are 'no marks for spelling'.
- We have found that in open courses, people new to training often like to come with a colleague. This gives them confidence but make sure that they meet others during the session by splitting them into different groups.
- Some groups of workers are not used to sitting and concentrating on ideas for long periods. It is useful to split the training into short bursts: for instance, two mornings instead of a whole day gives people a chance to reflect on things in between the sessions and is not so tiring.
- Coming to a new building as well as to a first course can be intimidating. Be there to welcome people as they come in.

Settling in

Working with new groups, you may find people who do not know how to 'behave' in a training session. Even with those who have participated on a previous course you will still come across individuals who do not see training in quite the same way as you do.

How long are we here for?

I was doing the introductions and asking them how they were feeling about the training as I knew they had been sent. 'What time can we get out?' was her reply. Deep down, I almost took it personally and felt rejected, but my head said, don't – the best way forward is humour and warmth. So I smiled and everyone laughed as I said: 'Thanks a million, I feel like your gaoler.' She was new to training and saw me as the 'teacher', the person with power. But at that point, she changed from being against to being with me.

At other times, I feel irritated when I'm asked: 'Can we have a shorter lunchtime and go early?' – particularly when I know the training is shorter than the normal working day. I believe that the quality of training is more important than the length and I'm often prepared to negotiate times. I also believe that the lunch break is important. You need time to digest physically and mentally. Three-quarters of an hour gives people time for this. Half an hour, in my opinion, does not.

Non-conformists

They came in dribs and drabs from the staff room. I had my notes, handouts, the flipchart ready and all the trainer's trappings. In the areas I work, I'm used to people coming in with cups of tea and coffee, but they arrived with a picnic – toast and marmalade, biscuits. 'We'll be having a break soon,' I said, 'then we can eat.' 'We know,' they replied, 'but we always have breakfast when we arrive and we haven't had time to eat it. We're always hungry here.'

GUIDELINES

- Negotiate timing at the beginning of a session. If you find later that you are going to run beyond the agreed finishing time, then let the participants know as soon as possible. It's best, though, to finish on time.
- Make it clear which times are approximate on the programme. For instance, breaks may be flexible, but starting and finishing times are not.
- Be clear about how long the break is. Sometimes important discussions go on during the break and you may want to be flexible. On the other

hand, you may have to chivvy people. One way to help people arrive back on time is to give both a time for starting back and the actual time for 'heads down and starting' (e.g. 11.25 for coming back, 11.30, heads down).

- Participants who are good timekeepers become very irritated when they have to wait. If you say you are going to start again at 2.00, then start, whether or not everyone is there. You can say something like, 'I'll restart at 2 – even if I'm talking to myself'.
- Give your views about time. If someone says, 'On the last course, the trainer let us have a very short lunch', then be clear why you prefer a longer break.
- With new participants you may be cast in the role of 'teacher'. You therefore need to discuss with them how you usually arrange matters. You don't want your words to be interpreted as: 'If you're good, you can go at . . .'.
- People who are not used to training can find sitting or concentrating for long periods very tiring. Build in short breaks so that people can walk round or have a quick drink or cigarette. Discourage eating and drinking during the actual training time, though you may judge it appropriate to allow people to bring in tea/coffee and biscuits at certain times.
- Be clear.

The truly terrified and recovering from a bad experience

You will have come across those who are extremely nervous either because they are very shy or because of a previous bad experience. Empathizing with them is important, and you may find that attending training regularly yourself helps you understand how it feels to be 'on the other side'. You are reminded of the importance of being a role model as a trainer, and you recognize how it feels as a participant to be in a group, speaking up, and being asked to do things. Most of us will probably remember some bad experience as trainees. We believe there is a difference between distress which inadvertently touches your personal feelings, and the distress caused by others leading to embarrassment or a loss of self-esteem. If the former is handled sensitively and appropriately, it can be helpful and cathartic. The latter leaves you with bad feelings and a reluctance to attend training again.

She had been fairly quiet throughout the training, but definitely attending. We were talking about supervision and the difficulties of receiving criticism at work. Then I noticed that she was putting her hands over her ears, watching me. She reminded me of a frightened child. I wanted to stop and say, 'There, there, it's all right' but only I could see this happening. This was not a counselling group. I felt disturbed, but I didn't want to treat her like a child. All I could do at that moment, I believed, was indicate with my face that I had seen and recognized her distress, but I had to go on. At the break, I took her on one side to talk. She was thankful that I hadn't stopped, said I had touched on an earlier experience for her, but that she did not want to talk further about it.

Had I done the right thing as a trainer?

GUIDELINES

- The role of the trainer is to create a safe atmosphere. An unambiguous 'formal' framework gives people boundaries within which to work together informally. People who are worried will recognize that everyone's opinions are valued and listened to.
- Check how people are feeling at the beginning, why they are attending, what they are expecting.
- Do not expect the truly terrified to speak up when they are in large groups, but give them opportunities to talk with one other or in a small group. Watch out for them and quietly check with them that everything is all right.
- Take people aside if you think they are worried or are finding things distressing.
- If people are distressed – and this can happen quite unexpectedly – give them time to cry or talk if they wish to, but avoid intervening to rescue them. Just allowing people to show and acknowledge their distress can be helpful.
- Remember you are a trainer and not a counsellor. If you believe that the person may need further help through counselling, then discuss this with them away from the group.
- Disclose how *you* feel, so that people are able to share their feelings with you or the group. However, make certain that you use this self-disclosure principally to help people move on.

The sleeper

Have you ever seen them wake themselves up with a snore? Watching someone's eyes gradually closing heavily and more frequently as you introduce your brilliant new idea is a depressing experience. Nevertheless, it is also satisfying to wake that person up and regain their interest and awareness with a lively activity.

Feeling sleepy in training is normal. At least, it's a common occurrence in stuffy or badly lit rooms. Also, a training day is a good chance for the team to go to the pub for lunch, and heavy lunches can wreak havoc. However marvellous the training is, people are likely to lose concentration occasionally. And those new to training and used to a job where they are on the go all day find sitting for a long time extremely tiring. Of course, there are also the passengers, who have just come for the rest.

GUIDELINES

- Accept that people may feel sleepy at certain points in the day. Warn the group, then they can let you know when they need a break or when it's happening to them.
- Work out the best moments of the day for introducing new ideas. Most people work best in the morning. Introducing a difficult new concept at the end of the day is not usually a good idea, but introducing a lively new activity to end the session on a positive note can be.
- Immediately after lunch is the usual 'siesta' time, so arrange for the participants to be doing something practical as soon as possible after lunch.
- Change the pace. If you feel people's concentration waning, you may say, 'We'll come back to this', and then move on quickly to another more energizing activity.
- There may well come a period in the day when you feel sleepy (see Chapter 6).
- Give people an opportunity to stand up and move about.

Energizing

Finding ways to stir your participants during their sleepier moments is a challenge. One way of energizing is to conduct a short activity that requires them to stand up and move about, though not too rigorously, especially if they've just eaten. The following example relates to time management but can be adapted for any subject area.

Ask the participants (a) to stand up and walk around the room and (b) to contemplate how pressured they feel at work. Stop them and say you want them to stand at a point on a scale from 1 to 10 across the room according to the degree of pressure they're experiencing.

		Acceptable pressure					Very pressured		
1	2	3	4	5	6	7	8	9	10
Relaxed					Pressured				More pressure than you can handle

Now ask them how pressured they like to feel in order to work effectively, and tell them to go and stand at that point on the scale.

In this activity you wake them up by making them change position, and there is likely to be some laughter too as they adjust their positions, change their minds, and generally get in each other's way.

Another ploy is to divide them up and move them into groups for the purpose of an activity. Here are two examples:

- Give everyone a number between 1 and 4. Ask all the 1s to swap seats, then all the 3s, and so on. Ask them then to work in pairs with the person now sitting next to them.
- Give each person a sticker in one of four different colours. Ask them then to make up a group with everyone wearing their colour, and to work in the four groups which are formed.

There are many ways of energizing, but we believe that the best methods relate directly to the training and help to move it forward. Games may be fun, but we are less inclined towards them if they have nothing to do with the training and can be viewed as wasting precious training time.

Distracters

The chairs are uncomfortable. It's too hot, too cold. They arrive late. They whisper to their neighbours and when you ask if they wish to disclose this to the group, they say, 'Oh, it was nothing interesting'. When you ask them to do something, they always ask further questions, make a remark.

Distracters – for this is what these people are – are often on the defensive. They are worried that you might make them look a fool, so they judge it best to make their move first – that is, throw the blame onto the trainer. They may distract deliberately to shift attention away from what they believe they cannot do, or they may be quite unaware of how distracting they are being. Usually they distract the rest of the group as well as you and the group sometimes deals with them for you.

> I was running a course on writing skills. We needed to refer back to a handout several times. Each time I asked people to look, she said 'I can't find it'. I felt my infant teacher voice coming on as I explained patiently again where to find it. But then I began to doubt myself – perhaps I hadn't arranged the handouts well – it should be easy to find them. I explained again where it was. As I was making a mental note to check them through so that it would be easier next time, one of her colleagues rounded on her: 'For goodness sake, surely you know where it is now.' From that moment she had no further difficulty.

The joker in the pack

Each time the discussion became involved or intense, he would crack a joke. This shifted the mood – as I'm sure he intended. The other participants would lose track, their thoughts and feelings interrupted at a crucial time. The third time it happened, I decided to be direct: 'I'd like you to stop doing that.' 'I'm sorry', he smiled. 'I don't want you to apologize, I want you to stop!' And he did.

GUIDELINES

- Learn to distinguish early between appropriate and inappropriate humour. First, the joker can be a positive influence, a real attribute to the group, using wit appropriately, providing adrenalin, tonic and relief. She or he acts as a counterbalance to the heavier training material or discussion. On the other hand, the joker could be someone who cannot manage her or his feelings, and simply cracks jokes whenever feelings are aroused – in other words, an avoidance mechanism. This is an inappropriate use of humour.
- Confront this latter use of humour head on. Ask the joker politely but clearly to stop it.
- Disclose how you, the trainer, are distracted by their joking at an inappropriate moment, though you welcome humour at more appropriate times.
- If you think the joker may have a serious difficulty managing his or her feelings, and that the joke is a disguise for fear, a way of expressing reluctance, talk to the individual privately during the break – find out what he or she wants from you in order to feel more at ease, less threatened.
- Find out whether the joker also wants some reassurance from the group. If so, encourage the individual to express his or her needs and feelings to the group.

Disappearing acts

The mobile rings – 'I'll be back, it's my son!' she shouts as she runs out. This may be marginally better than the person who without explanation leaves at the break and is never seen again. In both instances your concentration is broken, and you worry about the incident.

I was working with support staff in school. Someone came in with a message for one of the participants who apologized and left. 'What happened?' I asked on her return. 'I had to make the tea for the headteacher; she had important visitors.' I was not impressed and had words with the head afterwards. What message was she giving the staff about training and their own status?

Training on site has many pitfalls, unless there is a specific training room. Trying to work with a group who go back to their desks at every break to see what is happening can make you feel very marginalized. Yellow stickers are useful training equipment, but are not helpful when stuck to the door, encouraging participants to rush off to make phone calls, see people or sign letters whenever there's a 'quick moment'.

And then there are the people who bob in and out.

I had discussed the training with the new manager. She was keen to introduce some changes and wanted to be involved in the session with her staff so that she could hear their views. But as the morning progressed, she kept leaving the room on some pretext: she had to make a phone call, see someone, and so on. Each time she left, the staff glanced at each other and raised their eyes to the ceiling. This was not new behaviour for them.

I realized that she was feeling extremely uncomfortable. In theory, she wanted to be part of the discussion, but found it difficult to listen to ideas which were contrary to hers. I took her to one side and suggested that she either came in and stayed, or opted out. She chose the latter course and looked extremely relieved.

GUIDELINES

- Tell people what distracts you: for example, someone who continually talks to his or her neighbour.
- Ask people to turn off their phones or to let you know if they are likely to be called away on an emergency. Find out if there are people who have to leave the room or drink regularly for medical reasons.
- Ask people to let you know if they are leaving early, and let the group know if someone has had to leave.
- Explain the shape and thrust of the training. Endings are important, so if people are leaving early, the training may not feel complete.
- It may be difficult to stop the personal calls, but you may have some control over those to do with work.
- Training away from the actual workplace allows people to concentrate.
- When you set up the training, discuss the importance of people not being disturbed. This could be in the pre-course literature.
- Ask people to give themselves a break from their work at lunchtime, so that they are refreshed for the afternoon training session.

- If someone is so overwhelmed with work that she or he cannot concentrate, you may suggest they do not attend training at this particular time.
- If people need to return to their work after training, finish in time for them to do this before going home.
- Find out at the beginning whether any matters are preoccupying people. Sometimes a whole group may be distracted by something going on at work. You need to allow time to discuss this issue, and sometimes you have to abandon your programme altogether because of it. On other occasions, you can help people to put the issue aside and concentrate on training matters.
- Watch out for the distracters who are on the defensive. Make it clear that they will not be embarrassed in front of the group, but don't collude with them. Ask them to wait, allow others to speak. If they don't feel censured, they will begin to trust you.
- The group may point out how the distracter's behaviour is affecting them. Make sure that they do not laugh at or otherwise discomfort the individual in the process.
- If someone continually disrupts, remind them of the group agreement. You may take them to one side to discuss why they are disrupting, and in extreme cases, you may ask them to leave if they will not abide by the group agreement.

Activities

You've spent ages preparing, planning, devising. You've scanned every Gower manual, created scintillating exercises of your own, and you are pleased with yourself and eager to start – only to find that they don't want to do it! For all sorts of reasons, from shyness to snobbery, from feeling tired or challenged, and fearing to be shown up, to protests of it's 'artificial', 'silly', or 'pointless', so they make their excuses. Here we explore ways of understanding this type of reluctant trainee and encourage them to take part in the action. In view of the important role of practical activities in reaching objectives, we have set the scene and discussed options in more detail here than for some of the other areas we have covered.

Role play

Many of the group looked nervously about them as they entered the room. I took great care to create a sense of safety. Just as I was mentally congratulating myself on the relaxed atmosphere I had generated, there came the question, 'We're not going to role play, are we?' My heart sinks when this comes at the start of a session.

Where we stand on role play

The phrase 'role play' can trigger a whole gamut of negative emotions whenever it crops up, usually early in the session at the prospect of role-playing, or at the time you actually set up to 'role play', or both. If fears about role-playing emerge at the outset or later, then sensitively allay those fears as far as possible, otherwise they will affect participants' concentration and learning throughout the course. Anxieties about 'role play' and what you, the trainer, will expect them to do, can soon ripple round the whole group.

We make a distinction between 'role play', which we define as artificial situations specifically created for the group, and 'skills practice', which we favour and which involves real-life situations. These situations are preferably chosen by participants, or designed by you and based on pre-course discussions with participants, their manager, or others who have first-hand knowledge of the situations the staff do or could experience. In practising skills, participants apply skills acquired on the course to real life, and the process therefore has relevance and purpose.

Trainees often view 'role play' as irrelevant. Moreover, if someone has had a previous bad experience with role-playing on a different course, they may feel ill-disposed towards the prospect of more of the same and having to 'put on an act'. Conversely, it is the opportunity for the performer in the group to show off, put on a play, have fun, and shine as the centre of attention – but at the expense of learning and changing. Role play can turn into charades, but practice concerns the real world. The focus is on developing skills to handle situations more effectively.

If you opt for 'case studies', they must be relevant to the group. When you use a training pack, remember to adapt the case studies to the context in which you are training. The advantage of case studies is that participants are not asked to reveal their own circumstances, which can be difficult in front of colleagues. Yet once you introduce a situation, they may well respond, 'I can identify with that'. In our view, case studies are helpful for looking at how to handle situations, but not for 'role playing'. However, when you divide participants into small groups to examine case studies, you could suggest, 'You might like to try these out' or 'You might like to practise the situation to see what works'.

Another possibility is to ask them before the course to bring in their own case studies, which they can then discuss and practise either in syndicates or in plenary.

GUIDELINES

Fears at the outset

- Explain: 'We won't be doing any artificial role play. We'll practise skills and look at how to handle real-life situations so that you feel more able to manage them after the course.'
- Reassure the group about individual choice: 'There's no pressure on you to participate, you choose how you want to use the course.' Simultaneously, give them responsibility for their learning: 'But remember, the more you put into the course, the more you'll take out.'

Fears when you introduce practice

- Do all the above and more.
- Permit, even encourage, them to talk of their concerns, then validate the anxieties by acknowledging them. These concerns may include fear of exposure, being held up to ridicule, being criticized by peers and trainer, making mistakes and looking foolish, and never performing correctly. This openness helps them to understand that if they feel nervous, they are not alone.
- Be aware that the prospect is often much worse than the doing, and if you handle the early fears effectively, trainees usually practise with relish.
- Start by demonstrating a situation which most people could identify with and which might be fun. What better antidote to fear than laughter? You can use demonstrations to dual purpose, to relax the atmosphere and to show step by step how to practise.
- You could start by actively involving one or more participants who are particularly worried or cynical about the idea. If you can motivate them to participate and have fun as the centre of attention in the group, your battle for the hearts and minds of the whole group is practically won on this front.
- You might begin by deliberately making mistakes yourself in the demonstration, and then taking feedback from the group before having another go, this time taking the feedback into account and deciding what changes to make as a result in your practice. This shows participants the process, how to give and receive feedback, and how to incorporate it if appropriate into the next practice. Importantly, this process gives trainees tacit permission to make mistakes, before going on to do better, especially if they see the trainer caught out the first time! You will also have role-modelled a vital message: none of us is perfect all the time.

- When it is the participants' turn, make it clear that an Oscar-winning performance is not expected. There is the possibility of making a mistake and learning from it. Ask them to give feedback constructively, to listen to it, and choose what to use and what to put to one side. Encourage them to do, not simply to discuss.
- You could clarify that they need to practise the skills to meet course objectives.
- If the course involves assessment, explain the consequences: 'I won't be able to assess you fully if you don't do the exercise.'
- If participants are working in pairs, be aware that one person refusing to participate could hinder their partner in the exercise. The latter may not like to protest for fear of causing offence. In this case, you will need to intervene and explain to the person who is refusing to participate how their behaviour prevents their partner benefiting from the task set.
- If someone still refuses to do an exercise, don't force the issue. You can say, 'I do encourage you to have a go', and explain the benefits, but if they persist in their refusal, ensure that you enable their partner in the pair work to participate. You could say, 'I'll practise with your partner. How would you like to be the observer, and give feedback?' The objector is then involved and their comments valued – and once having participated as observer, they may well decide to practise. They may see the benefits and not want to be left out. Meanwhile, Person B has the opportunity to practise – with you! But do offer encouragement: they could feel anxious about practising with the trainer.

Summary

- Recognize that reluctance stems from many sources and expresses itself in diverse ways.
- Notice reluctance and check on the reasons for it without making judgements.
- If reluctance stems from anxiety, you can allay it with clear explanations and understanding.
- When people are angry, use that emotion as a positive force to look for solutions or creative ideas.
- Acknowledge that training is risky. People can feel exposed in role play, discussions and practical exercises. You can show them that it is worth taking the risk.
- Develop ways to involve people without forcing them.
- The most reluctant trainees at the start are often your closest allies

at the end, providing you have acknowledged and addressed their concerns.

10 The troublesome trainee

I may be glad to see the back of them when they go, but while they're there I'm really with them.

In this chapter we discuss people who are not necessarily reluctant – they might even be very participative – but aspects of whose behaviour cause problems. We shall review some ways in which trainers manage when they feel under attack or find a participant distracting.

Some participants are just plain troublesome. They are often the protesters, and they can be difficult. Although challenge is energizing and useful to a group when the questioner provokes thoughts and introduces new ideas, the protester does not challenge positively and can pull everyone into a downward spiral. He or she feels that they cannot achieve anything; there is no possibility of change. 'It's my manager who should be on this programme,' the person cries, 'then things would improve. I can't do anything about it.'

First, we consider what it is like to be in the firing line, and we suggest ways of responding and coping personally and professionally with the more caustic comments. Then we examine a range of awkward characters, from the self-opinionated to the 'teacher's pet', and we offer ideas and strategies in managing these. Finally, we imagine what it would be like if every group were perfectly behaved, without a protester in sight.

Thrown off balance

In the firing line

Attack can affect you mentally and physically and there is also the shock when it occurs unexpectedly. Participants sometimes seem to forget that you too have feelings. Challenge is stimulating and can be the stuff of training: it engages you and the group, and starts you all thinking. But an outright attack can be unnerving. You are caught off balance. Your immediate reaction is to attack back, yet you usually need to keep cool. Frequently, the attack has nothing to do with you, but it is hard not to take it personally, and when you do, the effect on you can be devastating. If you are new to training, it also undermines your confidence, and even if you are very experienced, it can be extremely hard to deal with.

So why are you attacked when you know that you are simply carrying out your role as trainer? You may perhaps have touched on a sore point for that particular participant or you may represent somebody or something they don't like. Some trainers have even been subjected to hatred for no apparent reason. You have to live through it somehow. A co-trainer can give you immediate support, but if you are on your own you will need good treatment for shock afterwards with a supportive colleague. We now explore some of the ways in which trainers have dealt with attacks.

'What a load of rubbish'

> From time to time I've been left speechless by the force and velocity of a nasty remark. For instance, I had been leading a discussion on a topic requiring considerable sensitivity when a man suddenly barked at me: 'This namby pamby lefty stuff is the ruin of our country! What a load of rubbish!' I had to be careful not to be drawn into the argument or to begin to doubt my own principles.

GUIDELINES

- Remind yourself that your approach is based on years of experience. It has been proven to work. People you've trained in these strategies have used them to great effect.
- Say that we have all had different experiences, and your learning was drawn from your experience.

'You're so muddled'

> Once a young woman yelled at me: 'You're so muddled. I don't understand anything you're saying.' It was halfway through the session, rather late in the day. If she had really not understood, why hadn't she asked earlier? She clearly wanted to undermine me and disrupt the group. At the time I said: 'Let's stop and talk about it. What would you like me to go over?' But the experience led me to review my own whole approach to ensure that this couldn't happen in future.

GUIDELINES

- Break up training into clear short sections.
- At the end of each section check with every participant that they have understood.
- Ask if they want more time on this section.
- Ask if they are happy to move on.
- Remember that participants are responsible for their own learning and this includes making clear to the trainer what their needs are. Give them the opportunity to do just this, regularly.

'This is crap'

I was training twenty teenagers, preparing them for the world of work. Ironically, we were exploring the personal qualities valued by employers when suddenly a young man banged both hands down on the table and shouted at the group and at me: 'This is crap, and you're crap!'

Had this happened to me when I was new to training, I think I would have been devastated. But years of experience has shown me that things are not always what they seem. By adopting an empathetic approach and taking the trouble to find out the truth, I discovered that his anger and frustration had nothing to do with me. He'd just been rejected for his dream job and he was seventeen today. Some cause for celebration!

GUIDELINES

- Don't take it personally.
- Recognize that their behaviour, though directed at you, may have nothing to do with you.
- Accept that genuine reasons may cause someone to be antagonistic to training or unable to learn at a particular time.
- Try to see, and to talk to, the good person behind the difficult behaviour.
- Ask them in a non-judgemental tone, 'Why do you call this crap?', repeating their words back to them, and then listen to their reply.
- If they don't have an answer, other than to repeat their disparaging remark, ask what they would like from the training that they feel they are not receiving. Encourage them to stay in the session.
- Be willing to listen and to offer to make changes, providing they are within the remit of the training.
- Refer them to the group contract, including giving feedback in a constructive manner and behaving respectfully in the group.
- If the behaviour continues and is affecting the group process and your

concentration, say something like: 'I'd have preferred you to stay and work within the group contract, but I'm feeling distracted and concerned that this will affect the objectives of the session. I suggest you go and have a coffee. I'll join you in the break and we'll see what we can resolve'. In other words, you are asking them to leave, politely and clearly, but without putting them down or using blaming language.

- Speak to the person privately in the break. Find out why she or he spoke as they did, and what would enable them to resume the training and feel more positive about it.
- If they come back, welcome them back. Give them the opportunity, agreed during the break, to say something to the group if they wish to. They might want to apologize!

Awkward characters

'In my opinion . . .'

While I don't delight in a shy, retiring group, I find no one more distracting than the self-opinionated know-it-all! Inside I seethe, holding my own tongue with difficulty.

GUIDELINES

- Acknowledge their experience or knowledge of a particular area – that is, validate it – before you say, 'I'd like to move on . . .'
- If they continue, speak to them privately so that they don't feel disparaged in front of the group.
- Be aware that this person could be challenged by others in the group who have the confidence to do so. In this case, encourage them to listen to each other and to find out what they want from each other.

'Something else I want to ask . . .'

One participant asked questions incessantly. I could see that others were irritated and I wondered if they were half as irritated as me. I answered politely at first, thinking the person was having teething troubles at the start of the course. He was like the young child asking 'Why . . . Why . . . Why?' If I continued to answer as I had at first I would never finish my material or meet the objectives. And I'd be colluding with his demands for attention at the expense of others.

GUIDELINES

- Keep calm externally, if not inside.
- Allow peer pressure to get people back on track before intervening yourself.
- Take the person aside at the coffee break and say something like: 'I understand that you want to know a lot, and I'm pleased you are showing such an interest. But some of your questions are taking us astray. I'd appreciate it if you could keep them to a minimum.'
- Use the opportunity of privacy to find out whether they are having any difficulties understanding the concepts or process, and, if so, what you could do differently to facilitate their learning.
- During the session, say, 'Let's put that question on hold and come back to it later if we have time'. Keep a flipchart or notebook of such questions and deal with them at an appropriate moment.
- If it's the manager asking these questions, and if you are feeling confident, point out respectfully that as they organized the training it would be very helpful if they behaved as a positive role model to the group. It is best to do this in private.

The pleaser

Some trainees do everything to please, wanting to be 'teacher's pet'. They keep offering to help, chat to me in the break or tell their personal stories to the group as a way of supporting the training. I find them hard to deal with precisely because they are well-meaning. Ironically, the effect is the opposite from what they intend: they bring red herrings into the session, the group is sidetracked, and I feel irritated.

GUIDELINES

- Remember that the occasional short story which supports your training may be interesting and enlightening.
- Draw the line when the short story starts to turn into a novel or the contributor tries to tell several stories.
- Be aware that other trainees may feel irritated towards that participant, and then towards you if you don't contain it.
- Other participants could rightly feel shortchanged, as the 'storyteller' is taking up chunks of time that they could be putting to good use elsewhere.
- Another participant may well intervene and say they'd like to get back to the course.

- If not, acknowledge the 'storyteller': 'I'm glad to hear you've found this approach so helpful. I'd like to move on now . . .'
- Tell the persistent storyteller: 'I can see you have some interesting experiences of this approach, but because of the objectives I want to meet within the time constraints of the course, I would like to ask you to put your stories on hold for now. If we have time later we can come back to them, or you might like to talk things over during the breaks.'

Distracting body language

One woman hadn't once looked directly at me – six weeks into the twenty-week course. I felt extremely uncomfortable and was convinced she didn't like me. I became more self-conscious, even averting my eyes when she averted hers – hardly good role-modelling from a trainer in confidence-building!

GUIDELINES

- Group members may feedback to the trainee, but if not, you will have to give feedback to them.
- Don't allow the situation to continue long enough to affect you.
- Choose an appropriate moment to address the matter. For example, in the above instance the trainer chose a session on body language and gave feedback to the trainee during a practical exercise.
- Draw minimum attention to the trainee so that they don't feel upset or embarrassed in front of others, for example, while you work with that person in a pair, or when they're in a pair and you are observer.
- Find out if they are aware of their behaviour, and why they look away while conversing.
- If she or he says that they have been taught that eye contact is rude, or that they feel too shy or embarrassed to look at people, explain to them the effect their behaviour has on you – that is, you feel awkward in their presence and wonder if they like you, when all the time it could be a cultural matter.
- Put them in the shoes of the person they are talking to in order to find out how they would feel. Ask them to imagine that they are talking to two others who are looking at each other but avoiding eye contact with them. How would they feel then? Probably excluded and rejected.
- Explain that when we speak and look away, our words lose impact and people don't take our views and feelings as seriously as we would like them to.
- Ask them to make an active attempt to give eye contact to you and

others in the group from now onwards, and ask if they would like you and others to gently encourage them from time to time.

Oh so laid back

The young man was so laid back, I half expected him to fall over! The way he sat sprawled across the chair, with a supercilious facial expression, his body language called out, 'I'm, oh so bored'. The trouble was, he had organized the training, so how could I criticize him? So I didn't, but I felt very awkward the whole three days I was there.

GUIDELINES

- Recognize that laid-back body language may be part of youth (or other) culture and nothing to do with the training itself.
- Find out the cause. Take them aside in the break and say, 'I thought you looked bored. Are you?' Check, 'How do you feel about the course? Is it as you expected?'
- If their response is negative, find out, 'What would you personally like that you don't feel you're receiving right now?' In other words, invite them to take responsibility for their needs being met, so that you can decide whether it's something you can cover. Show an interest and willingness to find solutions.
- Encourage them to participate more actively. Explain that they will take more out of the course the more they put into it.
- Tell them how you feel affected by them: 'I've been distracted by the way you appeared this morning and I'd appreciate it if you would sit upright and show that you're taking an interest.' In this fashion, you take responsibility for how you feel, rather than blaming them, and you ask them to change their behaviour.

An everyday tale of ordinary folk

Occasionally I've worked with a group where everyone is warm, welcoming, polite, understanding and keen to learn. I'm relaxed, they're relaxed. I think it's easy – but then I'm not so sure. As the day goes on, I muse: 'I've been here before and I'm bored.' I begin to think the unthinkable: I want the sniper to snipe, the shark to attack.

Having trained hundreds of sessions and thousands of trainees, I now regard the people I once dreaded when I was new to training as a challenge and source of inspiration. Conversely, the individuals I think I want – 'the ordinary folk' – when they're there, I'm not so sure anymore.

When the wittiest person is you, the most interesting tales your own, do you long for someone to wind you up and spur you on – that catalyst of dynamic and conflict?

Come back prisoner, come back protester, we need you!

Summary

- Remember that most trainers are goaded, sneered at and humiliated at some time in their careers – you are not alone.
- All too often, you have nothing to do with the participant's anger, but you do happen to be there, and so it falls on you.
- Take in all manner of comments, showing that you've heard them. Try to find out why they've been made.
- Keep your training goals in constant view so that you and they stay on track, or you can bring them back on track if they stray.
- Keep moving the training forward.
- When the going becomes difficult, console yourself with the thought that training would be very boring if people all conformed and never questioned anything you said.

11 Dynamic and conflict

It's when they're like nodding dogs in the backs of cars, going through the motions, that I feel depressed.

In this chapter, we consider how the group affects the training process for both the trainer and the participants, and we illustrate ways of channelling the dynamic and resolving conflict. First we cover situations where you are under attack from individuals or by the whole group, and then describe disagreements that can arise within the group. Finally, we discuss those individuals who are either rejected by other group members or who place themselves outside the group.

Motivating the group to work together is key to enhancing learning, especially in more interactive training such as communication skills. Yet the occasional storm is the norm, and as a trainer you will develop ways to control the situation, calm it, work with it or encourage the group to resolve the problem. Managed effectively, conflict is a valuable part of the learning process. Conflicts can emerge between two individuals, between groups, and between one or more individuals and you. Sometimes the whole group can turn against you.

The dynamic is always the unknown factor when you prepare for the training. We see the dynamic as the energy that moves a group forward or pulls it down. You may offer the same course to similar groups. From the very moment that one group comes together, you know that there will be questioning, a vitality and a connection between the participants even if they have not met before. Another group may take time to interact and you have to work hard to achieve this. Then there is the group who, for no apparent reason, just does not connect, and never demonstrates any real spark or energy. No matter how much effort you put into such a group, the return is negligible, and it is very difficult to maintain your enthusiasm. It's rather like pulling a jelly fish along on a piece of string. You go home exhausted and, even when the evaluations are positive, very dissatisfied.

You feel that you have missed something in the process, and that the group have not benefited fully.

As new trainers we found we shouldered much of the responsibility for what happened in the group, not fully recognizing its strength for resisting you or its potential for translating what you offer into something much more interesting. If you believe that training is about involving others in the learning process and using the group's knowledge and experience, then you cannot have complete control over what happens. You can inspire and motivate, help groups to focus, and move them on in their thinking, but you are not the fount of all knowledge – they have a great deal to offer too – and you cannot be the saviour that some groups look for. Certainly you are the hub of the wheel, central to what happens, but only one part of the whole. Although they may not acknowledge it, group members have power. They can choose to use you as the catalyst for change or they can do nothing at all about it. Moreover, they can use their power against you, and then you find yourself in the firing line.

It is not easy being a trainer, yet, as most trainers will tell you, it is the diversity of the work, the constant new challenges and the continual learning which keeps you there, keeps you fresh. You take risks, you find yourself in disagreements. Being asked in because there is a dilemma may mean that you highlight more conflicts. You find yourself blowing things open and uncovering a whole range of problems, but this in turn may lead to positive change and solutions.

You may dislike conflict and find it hard to manage in your personal life, but as a trainer, you recognize its potential for creativity and generating possibilities. You can use its energy to clear the air, start people talking and resolving long-term differences. You often look back on what seemed the most difficult training that you did and find it the most interesting and fulfilling. As one trainer put it:

> I feel better immediately someone engages with me. It doesn't matter if they say 'I don't agree'. From that moment, things start moving.

Turbulence: Disagreements with the trainer

The examples below describe the feelings trainers experience when anger and resentment is directed at them. Becoming the target of a group or individual's wrath for no apparent reason or because of something happening outside the training room, can temporarily confuse you, and can be extremely upsetting or annoying and, if it comes unexpectedly, a complete shock. Deliberately isolating yourself and adopting the position of 'heretic' or 'baddy' by asking questions which people would prefer not to hear, or by disagreeing with a group, requires confidence, particularly if you are training on your own. However, taking the risk and challenging positively is often an effective aid to learning.

We meet again

Having former colleagues or friends in the group can be very inhibiting, whether you have a good relationship with them or not, and you need to establish a clear framework with professional boundaries for the training. Those who know you well in another setting may find it hard to 'recognize' you in the trainer's role.

> I certainly wasn't expecting to see one of my old colleagues in the group – someone with whom I'd never enjoyed a good working relationship. He was now a manager. You can imagine my embarrassment and dread as the course was on managing conflict. I would never have agreed to do the training if I'd known he would be there, but I'd been asked to go in and replace someone else.

This trainer managed to talk privately to her old colleague before the training started. She established their respective roles carefully, congratulating him on his appointment and acknowledging his role as manager, and talking about how she worked as a trainer. Both assumed their 'professional' roles after this. This process is important with 'friends' too.

In-house trainers, who may sometimes take on another role in the organization, also have to establish their credibility. This will be enhanced where training departments have status and support within the organization.

Gang warfare

Sometimes it can feel as if the whole group is against you. You are blamed for matters which have nothing to do with you, and you have to withstand and deal with all this anger that is directed at you. Compulsory training for instance often generates this kind of group resentment.

> I worked in a large institution which was introducing a new scheme. Everybody had to attend one day's training. The adverse publicity beforehand compounded with anger about further changes had generated an enormous amount of resentment. I met them as they came in for coffee; they complained about the place, about the awful journey, and that this would be a wasted day for them. It wasn't an auspicious start and my opening welcome fell on stony ground.

The trainer goes on to describe how she had to call on all her reserves to deal with this group. She could have listened mainly to the loud voices, but instead she tuned in to those who were prepared to make the most of the day or who were not part of the 'gang'.

> The challenge was to offer good training and a positive day in the face of negative feelings. As trainer, I had to listen to the anger and resentment but not allow myself to be affected by it. It was a tough assignment. Fortunately, there were some people there who were prepared to be open, to leave their annoyance about the institution behind, and get on with developing their own skills. I concentrated on them, because I knew I couldn't win everybody over, nor was that my job.

There are of course times when the anger really is directed against you. You have to say something unpopular because you are the only person who can say what has to be said. People won't like this.

Traitor

If you are going to challenge, then be prepared for participants' anger and accept it.

> I realized that we couldn't move on until we had dealt with this issue, but each time I brought it up they backed off. So I had to challenge directly and say: 'You're avoiding this very important fact; unless we talk about it, there's no point in me being here.' They were furious, accusing me of not understanding and being unsympathetic. They didn't want to accept what I'd said, though they wanted to go on with the training after the break. They went on being angry with me, but because I'd actually let out the 'awful truth' they became much more open, and as the day progressed, I could feel us moving on. In the end, after the training, they were grateful that I had grasped the nettle. The manager later told me that there would probably have been a huge fracas between the group members if they hadn't thrown their anger at me. Fortunately, I'm broad-shouldered.

GUIDELINES

- If you find it difficult to invite a group's anger – and most of us don't go out of our way to make enemies – remember that challenge is an important device for stopping people in their tracks and encouraging them to think differently. Sometimes there is no alternative.

- If you challenge, it is vital that you do it about a specific issue and without aggression.
- When the group is angry with you, you don't have to go on the defensive. Listen to what they have to say, but hold your ground. While clearly acknowledging their anger, return to the issue you are discussing without becoming involved in a ding-dong argument.
- If you feel upset or exhausted afterwards, talk it through with a colleague.

Surprise tactics

Sometimes people seem to forget that behind your role as trainer is you. They abandon the social niceties, expecting you to accept their remarks without balking. Dealing with the shock when someone turns on you – or, as the following story illustrates, tries to enlist the rest of the group to gang up on you – is often quite enough to cope with. Therefore, responding appropriately, and remaining cool and confident is an additional professional challenge.

> The woman with the soft eyes leaned lovingly towards the group as the session drew to a close. 'I never dreamed I would meet such a wonderful group,' she told them. 'Thank you all so much.' She dropped her smile, leaned back and glared at me: 'As for you,' she spat at me, 'I'm miffed with you. You've completely ignored our expectations.' She acted as if she was speaking for the whole group. It was turning into gang warfare. She wanted them on her side, against me!
>
> So ended the first of two sessions on, ironically, 'dealing with difficult people'! Here was a real live difficult person for me to deal with. I was acutely aware of the importance of practising what I preach!
>
> I was shocked by this completely unexpected attack and aware of my incipient anger. I aim to meet course objectives and respond flexibly to groups and individual needs. I also always clarify what expectations I regard as outside the remit of the course and I felt that I had done so on this occasion. What else was I to do? It's a shock when someone feels such hatred that they try to turn the group against you: it is the old tactic of isolate, then attack.

This trainer had done everything that she could think of, but that isn't always guaranteed to satisfy everyone. Coming at the end of a session, an outburst like this can undermine you and leave you with a bitter taste, spoiling what has gone before. You have to concentrate hard on what you have achieved during the day.

In fact, aggressive outbursts may be more to do with the person than with you. Perhaps you have triggered a difficult emotion in them. Or they may be used to being 'the leader', in either a managerial or training capacity, and find it hard to accept that today you are doing the 'leading'.

GUIDELINES

- When under attack, ask the complainant to be specific: 'Could you tell me what expectations you would like met that you regard as unmet? Then I can ensure we cover them in the next session, provided that they're within the course objectives.' You may well find that they don't have any.
- Refer the participants back to the group agreement to speak on their own behalf and to give feedback constructively.
- Speak to the person privately, asking problem-solving questions: 'Why did you choose to object in the way you did? What precisely is it that you're unhappy with?' 'What can you do to make this course work better for you?' 'What would you like from me?' 'What would you like from others?'

The saboteur

Most of us have met the saboteur. Sabotage takes different forms. It can range from disagreement with everything you say to takeover in small groups, or to the general devaluing of discussions or exercises. It holds up the process, diminishes your confidence, and can be infuriating. The saboteur wants power or attention. You have to steer your way through the obstacles she or he puts in the way, and make a conscious effort to keep the group's needs and the training objectives in the forefront. This was difficult for the trainer below, where the saboteur struck immediately:

> I had been booked for a problem-solving session to brainstorm some new ideas. I had agreed the brief with the manager, and the starting point. This is important as these sessions are very intense in this business. I did my preparation, introduced the way of working which was new to some, and asked, as we had agreed beforehand, for the manager to start with the problem we had discussed. He started off with something completely different. The group of course didn't know what he'd done, but I felt mortified.

We have constantly emphasized the importance of agreeing a clear working framework, and this will always help you if the saboteur strikes. One trainer describes herself as holding the map – she points the way, stopping sometimes to agree on alternative routes or to look at a view more closely. The map gives the group safety. They can see the direction they are going in, even if they are not certain where they will end up. Sometimes she hands the map over to the group, but if they lose the way, she takes over again and consults the map. Ultimately, she holds onto it.

Stormy weather: Disagreements in the group

Disagreement between participants is not uncommon. According to trainer-speak, groups go through linear stages: they take time to form, the storm comes much later, only then do they truly perform. The reality is rarely so clear-cut.

Storms can come at any time. They brew, erupt, subside; they can be protracted or leave a sense of calm once the air has cleared. Some die down quickly, others turn into a cold war which outlives the training session. The training organizer or manager may have forecast the storm; on other occasions it will come as a complete surprise to everyone, including you.

The trainer helps individuals and subsets in the group to channel their energy constructively. After all, even where the will existed previously to find solutions, they may not have known how to go about this. The trainer does not resolve problems for the group, but empowers the group to take that responsibility for itself. The trainer mediates, teaches, guides, encourages.

It is precisely the energy that comes from difference of attitude, back-ground, experience, ideas and opinions that gives a group its dynamic – the cut and thrust that challenges and inspires both trainer and group. After the storm all parties might be better prepared to come to an under-standing of each other's roles and responsibilities, feelings and attitudes, and to be less judgemental and pejorative towards their peers and others.

Here we explore how differences emerge in the group and ways of handling them. First, we look at two warring factions, and secondly, at two individuals at loggerheads. Our third, fourth and fifth examples consider the dynamic created when the group rounds on an individual with or without reason, or vice versa. These include a view of the difficulties occasioned by judgemental and blaming attitudes within the group when this situation occurs.

In these examples, the trainer is not a party to conflict (at least not initially, though the way the trainer is perceived by the parties may change during the conflict). Consequently, she or he is in an excellent position as pacifier, diplomat and strategist.

Rising to the surface

A trainer told us how he relishes the challenge of facilitating participants of diverse experience and attitudes to reach a common understanding. He described how a deep breach existed between two factions in one of his groups. The storm, unbeknown to the trainer and probably even to the parties, had been brewing long before the session began.

> I felt as if I'd walked into a lion's den when I met these two groups of staff who had recently started working together. The two groups sat on opposite sides of the room. They sat quiet and expectant but I sensed danger. The morning went well. Through the exercises, the groups mixed, talked to each other and seemed to be making progress. But I was mistaken.
>
> After lunch, feeling we had set the scene, laid out where we were going, I posed the question: 'So how can we move forward from here?' That started it. The most vociferous member began. Another person who'd remained quiet until this point joined in. All the resentments of what had been going on emerged. I hadn't healed the breach – how I'd expected to in half a day with a few training exercises, I don't know. I realized that this clash needed to come. Up until now, everyone had been polite but restrained – now we were getting somewhere.
>
> The discussion began. It was evident that the two teams worked very differently. One group was used to discussing differences, and challenging, the other was resentful about what they believed was an imposition on the way they had worked previously. They felt threatened by the thought of this new group working closely with them and demanding changes.
>
> I was in the middle, fielding the responses, finding the questions. Some of the participants were shocked by the vehemence of people's views. Some were hurt and we had to look at this. But although it was a real humdinger, I was in fact pleased that the conflicting views had at last been well and truly aired. I hate conflict in my own life, but in the role of trainer, I can remain calm, outside the situation, and this, I'm sure, helps. I helped people to be clear in what they were articulating, to look at the reality of their situation, to find some ways of negotiating and moving forward. There was real energy in the group. The group managers had been worried about what was happening, but, as they said afterwards, turning the resentments into honest views meant they could start dealing with them.

You may not be aware of the latent antagonisms that exist, unless someone tells you beforehand. Often, as occurred in this example, the participants have not previously had the opportunity to meet face to face in order to think out and express what has been troubling them. However, it is not unusual for a trainer to find that there is a history of resentment between individuals in the group.

Here she goes again

In the previous story, it was the group who were antagonistic as a result of changes that affected them within the organization. The following story is about personal difference.

> I was training a group on their communication skills, how to be honest and direct, when I heard a woman muttering under her breath. It was loud enough to be heard: 'There she goes again.' This was aimed at a nervy young woman talking at length about her problems with others in the group. At this the nervy young woman leapt up, burst into tears and gulped, 'Typical – here *you* go again. Why don't you leave me alone?'
>
> I'd noticed they hadn't worked together in the group, but it was only when the sparks flew that I realized that there was a history of bad feeling between these two. I could also see from their colleagues' faces that this outburst came as no surprise, and one piped up, 'Why can't you two sort this out?' Perhaps this eruption was in itself a call for help to do exactly that.

While many people opt to avoid conflict at all costs, it's healthier for the parties concerned, the other participants and you to have it out in the open, rather than simmering under the surface. Either way, it will affect the group dynamic, but once it's out, there is at least a chance to resolve the issue and move on.

As the trainer, you have a difficult course to steer. You must not suppress conflict because you personally dislike it, but, on the other hand, you cannot allow it to take over the training. Therefore, you manage it as a part of the process in working towards your objectives. You recognize that ignoring it in the short term could adversely affect your training in the long term.

Try to diagnose and diffuse the emotions of the situation, and influence the disputants to take responsibility for their feelings and actions. You might ask them: 'What's going on here?' 'Does this concern your relationship in the office?' 'What do you want from each other?' Help them to look beyond the insults and blame to precisely what would make their relationship workable.

What they cannot resolve alone may well start to mend as they work together in the group, but if not, you will need to come to an agreement with them about how they will work together in the group, and remind them of the relevant part of the group contract. Then move on. Otherwise the dispute could take over and subvert your session.

I'm useless

Occasionally an entire group feels provoked by one individual. Not all the group express the provocation, which is often voiced by one angered individual who states how she or he feels, thus becoming the spokesperson for the group. A couple more may then find the courage to join in, and the rest will show agreement by nodding their heads.

> I'd asked them to role-play 'refusing an unreasonable request', and went to check how she was getting on. 'I'm useless at this,' she replied, which came as no surprise. Her sole contributions so far had been comments like 'I'm hopeless', 'I know you'll think I'm stupid', 'I'm pathetic'.
>
> Most of the group had been sympathetic at first, but as we went through the morning I noticed signs of irritation. Finally, her co-worker reached her limit: 'For goodness sake, why do you have to keep putting yourself down? I'm getting really irritated.'
>
> I was also irritated, partly because she kept droning on about herself in this way, but also because I just wished someone in the group would take her on, rather than leave it all to me. So I was pleased at the intervention, which takes courage on the part of a peer. At this point I also needed to mediate by checking how each of the participants felt, asking if they could now work more effectively together, and pointing out the courage they had both shown – one for speaking up, the other for listening to something that must have been painful for her to hear.

I do that

There are also groups that do not express their resentment. Everyone leaves the responsibility to someone else and eventually the trainer may have to intervene.

> 'Yes I do that too . . .', she said, for what felt like the hundredth time, before launching into yet another personal story. Another participant had been describing how she dealt with a difficult circumstance, only to be interrupted by this woman who was forever turning everyone else's story back to herself. She appeared quite unable to listen wholeheartedly to someone else. While the rest of the group did their best to empathize and offer objective suggestions, she could only relate experiences to herself.
>
> I could see the group frustration by their body language, but no one

said a thing. I hoped the group would take it on themselves to challenge, but they didn't. I knew I must intervene.

One trainer describes how he challenges such behaviour head on. He points out the hostility created and describes the offending behaviour: 'I think that you're provoking hostility in the group by interrupting and turning things back to yourself each time.' However, to do this you will need to be very confident and, if the sparks fly as a consequence, ready to calm matters down. On the other hand, the element of surprise, even shock, could make the participant realize the effect their behaviour is having on the rest of the group. You may choose instead, or as well as, to ask the interrupter to listen to others and speak only when it's their turn.

In any event, you must ensure that the group and the individual talk to each other about the cause of the hostility. If you leave it to simmer, the problem will surely boil over at an inappropriate moment.

GUIDELINES

- You can ask the group to talk about their feelings: 'How do you feel affected by . . .'
- You can let the conflict emerge and facilitate its solution. Both encourage and challenge them to clear the air: 'I'm glad you want to contribute but some people are unhappy about . . . and so am I. Why did you interrupt?' 'How do the rest of you feel?' 'What would you like from each other?' 'How do you suggest we sort this out?'
- You can give the individual the opportunity to explain, apologize and change.

Pointing fingers

Occasionally the group rounds on someone without justification.

He'd come on the second day, having entirely missed the first. I made a point of checking with the group that they felt fine having a newcomer join them, explaining to group and newcomer that this was because I recognized how groups develop a trust and it can be difficult for all concerned to accept someone mid-course. I allowed them time to think and talk, and they all gave their assent.

I was aghast when, at the afternoon break, I heard three of the group conferring in earnest: 'I wish he hadn't come.' 'Yes, I'm annoyed too.' 'I didn't want him here either.' 'He' was conveniently out of the room, out of earshot. I was enraged, but determined to keep cool as I confronted the trio. 'I'm disappointed to hear you talking about one of your group behind his back. I gave you time and opportunity to say you didn't want someone else to join today, but you said you felt fine about it. Why didn't you say something then?' I spoke calmly, and I hoped my voice sounded disappointed, but non-judgemental.

GUIDELINES

- Don't be surprised if you occasionally feel angry with some or all of the group. However you need to express that anger constructively and appropriately to effect the change that you hope for. Try gaining their acknowledgment that they could have behaved differently, and will work productively together for the rest of the course, abiding by the agreement.
- Where participants point fingers at others in their group, say that their behaviour is an example of the kind of indirect communication that creates conflict and resentment, and leaves difficulties unaddressed.
- As soon as anyone joins the group, refer them to the group agreement; new and old group members alike must observe it.
- Recognize where both your responsibility and the group's responsibility lie: ask participants to take responsibility for their own choices, and once made, to work with that choice.

Tyranny

We believe that all training must be set within a context of equal opportunities. It is a crucial part of the trainer's role to raise people's awareness and to present people in a positive light, whatever their colour, creed, gender, religion, disability or sexual orientation. Occasionally someone makes a belittling or offensive remark which we must not let pass, whether it was said intentionally or naïvely.

However, the trouble arises when an individual uses so-called political correctness, in such a way that it tyrannizes others: a tyranny of 'this is right and that is wrong', which allows no room for human error and the learning that can follow when people make mistakes. Such heavy handedness creates fear and defensiveness in the group. It is a barrier to open discussions and individual development.

You need to be fine-tuned to the language people use, draw attention to what is not acceptable, challenge it sensitively,[1] open up discussion about it, suggest alternatives. Adjectives like black, dumb or blind are often used pejoratively and you may want to suggest a preferred alternative when this happens; but it stops all dialogue when a participant angrily reproaches another for his or her use of a particular term, especially when the latter is simply out of touch with current word usage. Indeed, the accepted terminology itself constantly changes.[2] In other words, it is entirely different from where an individual is openly disparaging about, for example, women, black people or gay men and lesbians.

Semantics can, however, take over if you are not careful, and become an end in itself, more important than feelings and intentions. You have to expose people to changes in their thinking first, so that they want to change their language. We believe that it is comparatively easy to learn to change the language you use, but less easy to alter deep-seated attitudes and behaviour.

Odd ones out

Once in a while there is someone in the group whom no one wants to work with. It is not that the group is mean or nasty: rather that they may feel unsafe or threatened, as if that person is an intruder, and not part of their group. The body chemistry simply isn't there. Thus other members of the group seek to protect themselves against this intruder, choosing to work with those who will stimulate and give constructive feedback, to enable them to gain the best they can from the course. That, after all, is why they are there.

The sniffer

> The group winced as she entered the room. 'And I don't blame them,' I thought judgementally, despite having asked the group not to judge others harshly. 'Sorry I'm late,' she whispered – they usually are, the ones no one wants to work with. She was down at mouth, down at heel. Her nose was running with cold, and coming unprepared, she sniffed or wiped her nose on her sleeve in turn.

When first impressions trigger fear or distaste, and assumptions galore come into play, undoing the damage and helping the group to work cohesively becomes an uphill struggle. Whatever the outcome, it affects the whole group dynamic in the process.

You also have to cope with your own feelings, and no matter how professional you are, you are also human, with your own anxieties, fears and frailties.

Paramilitary man

> In he marched in his camouflage gear, heavy boots and tattooed snakes and skulls. Powerfully built and looking grim, he seemed decidedly out of place. He was two hours late, but on the list and expected. I felt the

group wanting to run away, and I would have been happy to follow. You could have cut the atmosphere with a knife.

GUIDELINES

- Allow yourself and others to be human – body chemistry, or lack of it, is a powerful factor in how we relate to each other. People have a right to like or dislike, take to or not take to, others.
- If the intruder is late, explain the key points of the group agreement and take them aside in the break to go through the rest.
- If they have colds or 'flu and are inconsiderately circulating their germs to the group, say you'd prefer them to get well first and book for a later date.
- No matter how challenging, eccentric, strange or threatening someone may look, give them a chance and they may present themselves very differently when they start to speak – thereby ensuring that the group also give them a chance.
- Putting people into small groups or pairs may break down those assumptions more quickly, as participants meet the person behind the mask.
- If it is clear that people are hostile to working in pairs with that person, aim for trios as a minimum number for group work.
- You could possibly work with that individual yourself during pair work, but remember that this separates them from the group, and also does not allow you breathing space, or others to get to know the person.
- When participants self-select their groups for group work, supervise sensitively to ensure that the outsider is not left out in the cold.
- Try not to allow your own assumptions and preconceptions to impinge: often the most difficult, hostile and unprepossessing characters develop and gel with the group in a most unexpected way. They may always be an 'outsider' in the deeper sense, but the group may come to work with and respect them despite a residue of discomfort. Paramilitary man turned out to be a gentle giant!
- If, however, that person is affecting the whole group dynamic adversely, and you personally feel affected as a trainer, your responsibility is to the majority of the group. In that case, you may have little choice but to ask them to leave.

Come again another day

It was the third week of a six-week course in personal growth. The participants had spent time contracting together, exploring their expectations and their fears, and building trust. A new participant asked to join. He seemed pleasant, and keen to be there. I couldn't bring myself to refuse, so I said fine. But it wasn't fine. He could never break into the circle of trust that the group had already created for themselves.

It was no reflection on him personally. Had he been there from the outset, I've no doubt he would have had a major role to play in the group. It was a stark reminder for me about the thrust and power of a group, how some groups are flexible and adaptable, while others, once formed, are sacrosanct and unwilling to entertain even the most potentially valuable new member.

GUIDELINES

- Ensure that everyone starts and finishes together. Everyone being present for the whole learning experience creates a climate of trust and mutual respect. The group develops a life of its own, and a kind of sanctity.
- The opening of any course is the origin of much of this trust, when agreements are made and individual objectives identified. The future of the course depends on the success of this opening.
- As the group develops together, anyone not in the group becomes an outsider – the member of staff who delivers a message, the person who brings the tea, the colleague who unwittingly puts their head round the door searching for a friend.
- If someone arrives late, find out why. They may have a very valid reason, such as a sick child to take to the doctor.
- If they have missed a key part of the course ask them to come back on another occasion, so that they can gain the full benefit of the training.
- Tell the person who arrives in the third week: 'We would have been pleased for you to join in the first week. But now the group has been working together and has built up trust, I'm not accepting anyone new, as it would be hard both for them and for you. Also, we've now covered important elements which you will now miss. Will you please book yourself on to the next date.'

In the above examples it is the group that has defined a participant as the outsider. In the following two situations, it is the individual or individuals who effectively put themselves outside the group of which they are supposed to be a part.

I'm not participating

It was the start of an interview skills course. I'd described it in the pre-course notes as being interactive, and told participants they would be expected to take turns to interview and be interviewed. We were all introducing ourselves and I was stunned when a man who was considerably older than the rest announced aggressively, 'I'm not participating'. I asked him why, to which he replied: 'Because I'm not. I learn by looking.'

This ran quite counter to the reason why people were there, and to the way that I work. I was totally confounded, especially as he'd asked to attend the course.

As in most awkward situations there is no one way of dealing with such an adamant stand, and what you do will also depend on your individual style of training and the guidelines available to you organizationally. You will need to be sensitive to the fact that some individuals are terrified of speaking up, of making fools of themselves, as they see it, in front of others, especially when they are senior in years or in status. Participation, however, does not entail exposing your innermost secrets, but rather putting forward your views, describing experiences when appropriate, and doing the practical work.

Nevertheless, the rest of the group may well feel uneasy if an individual implies that they simply want to listen and watch what's going on. After all, if everyone else is openly describing experiences and generously offering their ideas, they could object to the 'outsider' feeding off their input while contributing none of his or her own.

In these circumstances, you could find that it is a member of the group who takes up the challenge and tells this self-selected outsider that they feel uneasy about one of their number not participating. On the other hand, group members may feel that this person has a right to behave as they choose. Two factions may then emerge, one supporting and one opposing this individual. In a less confident group, there may be no spoken objections, but you will still sense that they exist. This is particularly likely when the group have only just come together. You need to find a modus vivendi quickly, otherwise this issue could dominate the session.

GUIDELINES

Here are some possible ways of managing the situation:

- To try to prevent the situation arising, state in the information supplied to participants before the course that they will be required to participate.
- When you make a group agreement at the beginning, include participation. You could also give people the right to choose not to participate,

but if so, you would like them to explain their reasons to the group. You can refer to the group agreement during the course.

- Ask the individual if there are ways in which they will want to participate.
- Explain that the more they put into the training, the more they will benefit from it; hence not participating will limit their learning.
- If you see once you start that the group is adversely affected by this situation, take the person aside during the break, explain the effect on the group of their behaviour, and ask again if they are willing to start participating.
- Give them the option to change but clearly set a time limit for it: 'It's having an adverse effect on the group. If you don't feel able to become involved once we return after lunch, I'll have no option but to ask you to leave.' Or on a longer course you might suggest, 'Let's review the position at the end of the day'.

However, you have a duty to look after yourself as well as your participants. You won't know what they are thinking or learning if they don't participate, or even whether they understand what you are teaching them. You are being watched over silently, and silence can be very powerful. What effect will this person's behaviour have on you and the quality of training you deliver?

The purpose of group work is not essentially to give maximum support to the neediest individual, the attention seeker, the awkward and the disruptive. Moreover your duty as their trainer is to the majority who want to learn and co-operate, albeit within a framework that allows them to challenge you. In extreme circumstances where you and/or the group are affected by an individual's behaviour, to the extent that it is felt or perceived to be threatening, you have a responsibility and a duty to ask that individual to leave.

Some organizational cultures will not permit you to do this, and you may then find yourself caught between the rules of the organization, the behaviour of the individual, the benefit of the group, and your own judgement as a trainer (see Chapter 7).

Summary

We have given examples of groups that are fragmented and find it hard to work together or with you. But the dynamic or energy of the group can operate in your favour and transform the training into something exciting and exhilarating for both you and the participants.

- Challenging participants positively is part of your role as trainer. You can be the catalyst for change and for new ways of thinking.
- Be prepared for participants' anger, which can erupt without warning. You are not there to fight or counterattack. Be accepting, but without becoming defensive. Concentrate on the issues under discussion, so that participants use their anger creatively, not destructively, as a force for change.
- Recognize your role as mediator and referee. Give participants opportunities to try things out and hear your 'objective' view.
- Use differences positively – participants can learn from them. Challenge without becoming embroiled in a battle.
- Recognize that participants may find conflict and differences uncomfortable to manage when they occur in the group. Contain the situation and encourage them to discuss the issue without blaming or judging each other.
- You may be left with very troubled feelings after attacks from individuals or groups. Once outside the course, ensure that you are not left to brood on this alone. Speak to people you trust about your experiences and feelings.
- The most challenging or difficult moments often provide you with good material to learn from, as well as memorable stories for later. But don't forget, when you talk about participants, don't break confidentiality – keep their names and identities anonymous.

Notes

1   You might sensitively challenge a comment like 'Everything looks so black' with 'I prefer to say *everything looks bleak*'. Explain that you discourage the pejorative use of the word 'black', and do this without blaming the speaker or putting them down.
2   The change in use of words from 'retarded' to 'mental handicap' to 'learning disability' is one example of this. By the time this book is published it may have changed again. We believe it is the people referred to who are best placed to decide on the preferred language.

12 A question of balance

You want them to talk, but there comes a point when you want them to stop.

The challenge for the trainer is to strike a balance between encouraging contributions and not allowing individuals to take over. The stories in this chapter illustrate how individuals, sometimes unwittingly, disturb both the group's balance and your own. We look, first, at people who may be anxious or upset and how they can express these feelings appropriately but not at other people's expense. Next, we consider the different ways in which people steal attention: they may find themselves cast as the group's idol; they may draw attention to themselves by their behaviour or they may deliberately set themselves apart. After commenting upon the sexual dynamics within groups and how to avoid stereotypical behaviour, we end the chapter by exploring the kind of group that bring out the best in you and others.

Distress signals

People display their distress in different ways, sometimes openly through crying, or by becoming angry and defensive, or through non-verbal signs. They can feel anxious whatever the course. The non-verbal signs are important, as an IT trainer explains:

> People often feel that they will be made to look a fool on IT courses. For example, I was in very early preparing for work when a woman looking very nervous arrived. I welcomed her into the room and began to talk to her. 'Will we be able to ask questions – we weren't able to on the last course?' 'But of course,' I said, and she immediately began to relax.

Some behaviours irritate although they are not intended to do so and may be symptoms of anxiety, stress or overwork. You may also inadvertently trigger off an even greater level of distress.

> I was dumbstruck when she burst into tears. I thought I was asking the group to do something positive, something light-hearted. I'd asked everyone to talk about something they took pride in. I didn't know what to do.
>
> Many years on, I now know not to be surprised at who becomes distressed, or at what point in a course. It can be men or women, young or old, managers or people who see themselves at the bottom of the ladder. People are people and they all have frailties, whatever their standing. Training which touches a raw nerve, the experience of being in a supportive, empathetic group, having time to think things over, all can contribute to emotions being expressed which may have been suppressed or bubbling beneath the surface.

The need to manage distress within the group is most likely to arise during personal growth training, but it could arise unexpectedly during other types of training. If you work in a field such as assertiveness, counselling or managing stress, you are more likely to have received training in handling difficult emotions and their effect on the group as a whole. You may, however, experience difficulty in dealing with the situation. You have to find ways of managing your own discomfort, as well as that of the individual and the group.

GUIDELINES

You must take into account the following considerations:

- If you make a contract with participants, say that it's fine for them to express how they feel. As a way of giving permission as well as encouragement to your participants, you can role model this by disclosing times when you yourself have felt vulnerable. In other words, you too have had your difficulties but now you're up there training.
- In personal growth training your approach may be therapeutic and have a therapeutic effect, but it isn't therapy, it's training. So don't actively encourage people to dig too deep. If they start digging deeper than you feel is a comfortable level, remind them that you are there as a trainer, and you cannot deal at length with individual needs. Remember that your responsibility is to facilitate learning, not to counsel.
- Value the distress, don't ignore, dismiss or ride roughshod over it. For

example, you could say: 'This seems like a deep personal issue. It's not the place here to explore it in depth, but at the end of the course I'd like you to feel you have a way of following it up.' In many cases, you will want to encourage them to have faith in how resourceful they are.

- Don't rescue or pity the person, and don't allow others to do so. He or she may be distressed but is not automatically a victim, and rescue or pity can disempower and lower them even further. Be aware that the need to leap in with 'There, there, don't cry, it will all turn out all right', says more about the person uttering it than the person in distress. It means in effect 'I can't cope with someone crying, so I'll stop them'.

- In normal circumstances, don't permit someone who is distressed to hijack the course so that they take up the time and the attention of the rest of the group, who all start to support that one participant in the belief that his or her situation is worse than their own.' It is, however, occasionally appropriate in a course that continues over a long period and where a session or large part of it is devoted to the issues of one person.

- Giving time to an individual is appropriate in some fields of training, such as interpersonal skills, confidence building or stress management. You can always use pair work as a way of giving people more one-to-one time.

- Check at the end how the individual feels, and help them find professional help if that's what they want. Carry with you names and telephone numbers of appropriate individuals and organizations, or be ready to provide them after the course. Any conversation about this matter must be conducted in private and in confidence.

- If the training you do is more of a personal than technical nature, you may find it helpful to work continually on your own personal development, through training and counselling. If you can heal your own hurts you are more likely to be able to respond both sensitively and constructively when others are hurting.

Certain people

The stars

Some groups have their idols. Participants look up to them, depend on them, expect them to have the answers. This inhibits the training both for them and for the idols.

In our business there are the stars. Their peers see them as gods because they bring in business, make money. They think that the stars have all the answers and possess some kind of 'magic wand' and that the training will give them an easy way to find more clients and business.

Sometimes these 'stars' are unpleasant people, while at other times they're terrific to train. The point is, everyone listens to them. As I'm also part of the business I have to tread carefully – I need them on my side, but I also have to take the spotlight off them. The 'stars' don't necessarily want to be seen as the source of all knowledge. Usually, they have come on the training because they want something from it for themselves.

It is your role to question or enhance what the stars are doing, using their experience, but putting it into a context where others can see how they also can achieve. Emphasize examples of the stars' hard work or good interpersonal skills. Demonstrate to the others that although these people may have a particular talent or personality which brings them business, there is no 'magic' way. Above all, take the stars out of the limelight, acknowledging their success but also giving them a chance to benefit personally from the training. At the same time, make the other participants concentrate on strategies and alternatives for doing the work in a way that suits them.

Mr or Ms Technical

They know the inside of a duck's backside. I realize that it's good to have keen people on the course, but Mr or Ms Technical want to know every detail. They have you going off on tangents if you're not careful or wondering whether you know all you should.

Other participants easily become bored when someone wants to discuss minute details or to analyse every point. Yet these people are often very enthusiastic, if not always correctly focused. The main objective is not to dampen their enthusiasm or interest. Acknowledge that they know a lot, but help them to channel their interest on to the specific subject in hand. Suggest ways that they can find further information or explore the subject outside the training room.

The life historian

We all meet them. 'Ah yes,' they say, 'that's happened to me', or 'What I think . . .' and then they launch into a long story. As it goes on you look for the point which you can pick on and so bring their story to a close. You see them in small groups, mesmerizing others who haven't managed to get a word in edgeways.

You may well have agreed in your group contract to listen to each other, to respect each others' views, but the anecdotal participant can take this to the extreme. They are oblivious of their responsibility to others.

Politely but firmly ask the talker to spell out the main point they want to make or tell them that you must move on to the next person or subject. Sum up briefly what they are saying, but never say you will come back to their story later unless you actually plan to do so. If they persist, interrupt straight away. Say thank you, but repeat that you need to hear from others too, and then deliberately move on.

Before you start a small group exercise, stress that you want to concentrate on the question and to avoid anecdotes. If necessary, give an example of the difference between an anecdote and a relevant experience. If you see a small group being taken down an anecdotal route, go over, join in quietly and move the group back on track. Other participants will be most grateful.

Finally, learn from your experience of being on the receiving end of the anecdotal and use your 'stories' to illustrate a point carefully and sparingly.

The caucus

I noticed in the second week of a ten-week course that three people always worked together, like their own subset or caucus. When I asked them to work with others they flatly refused. That caused an inner conflict for me: 'Do I spend time on this, or is it my responsibility to the rest of the group to move on?' In a course which includes listening and empathy, could I allow a caucus to refuse to listen and empathize with others?

GUIDELINES

- Try to prevent caucusing by contracting with the group at the outset to work with different people throughout the course, and by asking participants not to be judgemental towards people who are different from them.
- When you divide them for group activities suggest that they work each time with someone new. One way to start is to draw lots so that they don't have to choose.
- Recognize that once a subset has formed it could be difficult to separate. They feel safe together and don't quite fit into the rest of the group. Others in the group may feel angry or offended at their refusal to work with them.
- Have the courage to be explicit. You could say to the subset: 'You are setting yourselves aside from the group, and depriving yourself of the benefit of input from others. What benefits do you think you could gain from others?' Let them deduce the benefits for themselves.

- Check with the subset why they have separated themselves. You could ask: 'Why do you feel you want to keep together?' 'What is it you're worried about in working with others?' 'What would help to make it safe for you?'
- You may choose to talk to them in their subset before opening the topic to the whole group. You could check with the whole group: 'How do the rest of you feel about what's happening in the group?', and ask problem-solving question like 'How can you make this safe for you all to work together?'
- Try a bridge-building exercise. Explain that in our relationships we have to find ways of relating to people we don't empathize with, and even dislike. Ask how they can do that?
- You may choose to exert your authority as a trainer, acknowledging the difficulty for the subset, while requesting them to co-operate. 'I know this might feel like a challenge for you, but I would like you to work with everyone in the group from now on.' The subset's behaviour could be their way of challenging their leader – you! They could refuse, but nothing ventured, nothing gained.
- If the course is accredited, be clear with the subset that you will not be able to assess them fully if they do not cooperate in the group.

Gender and the trainer

No sex please, we're training

The female trainer's tale

> Everything about the very young man was saying, 'I'm a man, you're a woman', yet he never spoke. His clothes, the way he moved in his seat, ran his fingers through his hair and stroked his jacket showed how sexually aware he was of himself and others. It was as if he was trying to intimidate and undermine by implying I was a sex object, nothing else. I didn't know what to do, so I ignored it – that is, I didn't do anything about it. I thought that if I confronted him he'd probably say, 'That's wishful thinking', and imply it was my fantasy.

The sexual dynamics between members of the group and you, or between the trainees themselves, can skew what you are trying to do or stop people taking things seriously. Verbal sparring, for instance, can be fun, but when it turns into flirtatiousness, then you have to take action.

Looking good

Young female trainers who look younger than they are have to prove their credibility quickly and be taken seriously. The ones we interviewed all said they consciously avoid looking sexy: 'Men might look at my legs instead of concentrating on what I'm doing.'

Women to the rescue

Older women trainers suggest how easy it is to find yourself cast in the mothering role. You must also be careful not to cast yourself in it.

> The one man in the group arrived late, for which he had a good reason. My co-trainer rose to greet him but then I watched with horror as she fussed round him, fetching him coffee and drawing attention to his arrival. She realized what she'd done afterwards. She's a kindly mother and he was the same age as her son.

Men and women co-training need to discuss their role modelling to the group before the session. It's important not to slip into stereotypes.

Men to the rescue

> I was working on gender issues with a mixed group. To my annoyance I was right in the middle of introducing a complex and sensitive matter when I was interrupted by three men, one after the other in quick succession. I wanted the group to notice and manage what was going on. But before anyone had a chance to challenge, in leapt my male co-trainer, now the fourth man in a row to interrupt me. Men to the rescue! 'I was only trying to be helpful,' he explained.

People need to hear men and women speaking up or challenging for each other, so it's not always the woman who speaks on women's issues and vice versa. This is very different from rescuing or defending each other.

Stereotyped

Women participants may react angrily because they 'resent being told what to do by a man'. Woman trainers who are controversial can find themselves typecast as anti-men or militant feminists. You then find yourself stereotyped. A trainer working on gender issues, but with men only, says:

> I have to avoid being seen as a stereotypical feminist. I do get cross,

but I have to be subtle. What I do is design the exercises so that participants have to face the facts. They find themselves in a position where they are arguing out the position together.

Assumptions

Groups can easily make assumptions about each other, and such assumptions must be highlighted at once by making people think about what they are saying, without putting the onus on anybody – as, for instance, in the case of the trainer who quietly said: 'We're making assumptions in this room that no one is gay.'

It is easy for people to be cast by others in a particular role. A lone woman in a group, for example, may have difficulty in speaking up, but this may only be because of the way the group is set up or the way they respond to her. Given the opportunity, and by you changing the dynamic or the framework, her voice may be heard easily. Similarly, a lone man may find himself typecast, but he may actually be feeling intimidated or self-conscious, or be too aware of a need always to say the 'right' thing.

Furthermore, if there is a lone representative, make sure he or she is not pushed into being the spokesperson for their particular group. No one can speak on behalf of all men, women, gays and lesbians, people with disabilities, black or white. He or she is entitled to his or her own views.

Colluding with the culture

Both men and women trainers have to deal with trainees who seek attention by using their sexuality, playing, for instance, the helpless woman or the macho man. You have to watch carefully too for the games that go on in the small groups. If it is the men who always give feedback, it could be that they tend to take over or offer to do it, but it may also be because the women let them or expect them to take the lead.

Often you will find that men and women feel safer and are more honest in a same-sex group. But even then, you have to make sure that you don't collude with a particular culture, such as women blaming men for all the ills of the world or men taking traditional female roles for granted. You also need to notice the power relations. When you are training senior executives they are likely to be mainly men, when the course is for administrative staff it is likely to be women. As trainer, you have the power to question these circumstances. Your course may not be specifically about gender issues, but you can help people to examine different points of view or not take everything for granted.

Sunny climes: groups that work

You carry most of the responsibility for uniting a group, by creating a safe, listening environment, treating people as individuals, and being aware of different needs or rates of learning. You draw out the commonalities, allow room for differences, and resolve difficulties, tuning in to the feelings of the group.

In addition, groups that work well together have the following characteristics:

- A trust and appreciation of you and of each other.
- A sense of equality as human beings, even though they may have hierarchical or social differences. Thus they can be honest and down to earth with each other.
- An understanding from regularly working together, or a freshness and interest in new people.
- An acceptance of their own and others' strengths and weaknesses.
- A readiness to take on new ideas and opportunities, and to learn from them.
- Humour and an ability to laugh at themselves and with others.
- Compassion and self-awareness.

Sometimes one or two individuals start with these qualities above and imbue others in the group with them. Certainly, when you do have these qualities in the group, then, as the trainer below describes, the training takes on an extra quality.

The cook, the cleaner and the financial director

One of the most exciting groups I ever worked with could not have been more disparate. The participants had all chosen to come, and I knew that I could adapt the subject matter so they would each find something personally relevant. But as they introduced themselves, I began to wonder how they would manage together, for they came from very diverse cultural, social and educational backgrounds.

Analysing later why it worked so well, I realized that people were ready to trust me very quickly and that this trust radiated out to each other. There was more to it than that, however. One person had a particular charisma and group skills – which I think she was completely unaware of – that bound people together. She got to know people quickly, and listened to and remembered what they were saying. The whole group followed her example.

People were very interested in each other. Their differences of background and approach helped them to look at things in a fresh way. There was a common concern to find solutions which were relevant to others' questions and issues. They were genuinely pleased when their suggestions helped others to find their own particular way forward. There was no competition and a great deal of humour. We all came away feeling valued and with renewed faith in humanity.

Summary

The theme of this book has been the troubles you have to face as a trainer, but as the last story illustrates, it is not all bad news. Variety in a group is generally constructive and individuals enhance your experience and skills with theirs and enrich the training process. Your role is to interweave their contributions with yours, so that the training and materials feel pertinent and significant to the specific circumstances.

- Ask for differing views and opinions. Develop an environment in which individuals can express their differences without fear of being put down. Use this safety to develop an openness and interest in finding ways of resolving problems and issues.
- Let individuals take the lead on occasions, but remember that your first responsibility is to the group. They will expect you to act when someone takes over or dominates.
- Listen to the participants' personal demands but don't allow these to interfere with relevant course material or change the main objectives of the training.
- Draw participants' attention to what is happening, so avoiding any scapegoating or colluding with stereotyping. Individuals can easily find themselves labelled either before or during the training.
- Keeping a balance between what the majority wants and what individuals want sometimes means that you can't please everyone. When participants are quite clear about what to expect from the course, you will be better able to maintain that balance.
- Set up support systems for yourself personally and professionally. Join a group of trainers through people you know or a professional organization. Talk through ways of handling situations. Turn to them also, as a group or singly, and seek help and advice on those days when people have upset the balance.

13 Tales of the unexpected

What you can predict about training is its unpredictability

Do you ever think 'I bet this never happens to anyone else'. Think again. In this chapter we offer some 'tales of the unexpected' told to us by trainers, both new and experienced. The message is simple: 'Don't worry. It may have happened to you, but you are not alone.' Experience, know-how, confidence, tenacity and an overriding sense of humour will see you through during even the most difficult days.

The stories they tell

Intruders

The boy with a bucket on his head

> A small boy with a bucket on his head suddenly appeared and rushed across the room. The crèche was supposed to be next door. We were well into the session and I was demonstrating the importance of saying things clearly and assertively. At last – the real test. Could I as the trainer, with credentials of working with children and adults, demonstrate clear assertive communication with a three-year-old?

Back and forth

> We had just settled down for a serious discussion. Everything was quiet when a woman walked straight through the room. 'Morning,' she called out heartily. 'I'm just on my way to the garden.' We settled in again but

157

as if one disturbance wasn't enough, she came back again ten minutes later. 'Bye now, everyone,' she said.

Who have we here, or better late than never

The induction course was running in the same building as several others. There were 35 new staff and we asked them to introduce the person next to them. They had had a discussion together about when they'd joined. We were over halfway through the feedback when someone introduced Janet: 'She's been here 17 years.'

Is this philosophy?

We were an hour into a course, exploring the impact of human behaviour. An elderly woman suddenly intervened. 'Is this philosophy?' she asked. 'No,' I replied. 'It's assertiveness.' 'I booked philosophy,' she said, 'but this is wonderful. I'll stay, if that's all right.' It was. She did.

It was a warm, funny experience, and though we laughed at the time, it taught me to check at the start of a session that everyone there is on the right course, that the names on my list are the people in the room, and to note names of new people and replacements.

Interruptions

Safety first

She arrived at the break time in the afternoon. 'Have you been doing a report-writing course?' she asked. I had, all day. 'Oh,' she said, 'I've just realized that's the course I was supposed to be on today. I've been next door doing First Aid. I thought it couldn't be right because I was the only admin person there.'

Everybody out

We were discussing how to enter a room with confidence. I encouraged them not to be apologetic about it. If they were, they wouldn't be taken so seriously, as when someone says, 'Sorry to disturb you'. At that point someone tapped on the training room door, saying, 'Sorry to disturb you. Please evacuate the building. There's a bomb scare.' The group sat there ready to continue – they thought it was part of the course. But it was a real alert!

Distractions

As if you don't have enough to think about, there are always other things going on.

Stalkers

> I swear there is a phantom driller, alternating between hand and pneumatic drills, who follows me from client to client. Participants love them, I hate them.

Carry on training

> I didn't take any notice of him, but at the break I went up to him and said: 'I'm sorry if you're finding this rather boring.' 'What makes you think that?' he asked. 'Seeing you reading the paper and eating a Crunchie bar,' I replied. 'Oh, don't you worry about me, dear, you just carry on.'

Hideaways

> Have you ever noticed that the ones who 'know it all' sit at the corners of the group? It's so they can hide and then pop out with their statements of 'fact'.

Knitting patterns

> I found it hard not to smile when she took out her knitting at the start of every session. To give her her due, she did finish the garment by the end of the course.

Personal problems

As others see you

> I was booked for the second day of the course, and had come to stay the night at the training centre. At 3 a.m. the fire alarm went off. I met the participants in the drive and we waited huddled in our nightclothes for half an hour while the fire engines arrived and checked everything for a false alarm. You can imagine the start of the course at 9 a.m. They'd already seen me as I really am – and talk about a dip in the day.

Buttoned up

The venue was some distance away, so the company arranged for me to spend the night before in a hotel. Making the best of myself in the morning, I succeeded in splashing mascara all down my yellow suit. As they were the only clothes I had with me, I'd no choice but to wear them. So I kept my jacket on all day, buttoned up. I was so hot and I so wanted to look cool. Now when I train away from home, I take a second set of clothes.

Never again

I once worked at a venue with no water, and no toilets.

Birth pangs

I recall going back to training only 12 weeks after giving birth. It was just my luck that the first venue I worked in had nowhere private I could go to express breast milk. I was reduced to lurking in the store cupboard next to the training room juggling my electric pump. Anything was better than going through the day in agony.

Credentials

Watch out, the trainer's about

I was introduced to the group by someone who'd quickly read some notes about me beforehand. I was doing some work about the Children Act so I was horrified when, after he'd given my credentials, he said with a smirk, ' . . . and she's an assertiveness trainer, so you'd better be careful!'

A high price to pay

I was 15 years younger than the youngest in the group and new to training. I had been asked to do a day on presentations, and, although I'd done a good deal of preparation and research, I had had a sleepless night beforehand. People were introducing themselves and saying what they wanted to achieve from the course. He said: 'I'm the chairman and I've just come in from abroad. I'm here to find out what original ideas you have that I haven't heard a thousand times before.' I said, 'You're not paying me enough for me to come up with original ideas. They're very rare. What I hope is that you'll hear a new slant on an old one.'

Psychology

'Are you using Freud's, Eysenck's or Jung's material?' For a moment I looked aghast, feeling caught out and ignorant. 'Actually I'm using my own,' I replied.

Patience is a virtue

I have amazing patience when I train. I'm sure that it's because I had a difficult mother and I learnt to listen to irrelevancies.

High-tech

Take no notice

The participants were videoed for a presentation course. They received feedback, and then an opportunity to come back and try again. One of them who hadn't done very well went home rather depressed and showed the video to his wife. 'I think you're marvellous,' she said. 'Don't take any notice of them.' To give him his credit, he came back, made a much better presentation and later told us what she'd said.

Hackers

There are heaps of opportunities for practical jokes in IT. You name it, I've heard it. One clever clogs computer hacker converted all error messages into expletives. We all had a good laugh before I called the group back to business and suggested they move on. You have to respect your delegates' skills and integrity! Once you cease to have fun, it's time to stop training.

A quick exit

A heavy load of luggage

I'm not satisfied with this course and I don't want you to see the evaluation. I'm sending it direct to the Training Department.' He clearly meant to sound threatening but I felt irritated as he tried to wield power over me. I said, 'If you don't explain why you're dissatisfied, there's nothing I can do about it,' but I thought, 'Go and take your baggage on the next train out of Waterloo.' As a new trainer I'd have been worried, as an experienced one I can't be bothered with that type of behaviour.

Saved by the bell

I had had what felt like an appalling day's training. I was dreading the evaluation. At 4.30 p.m. the fire alarm went off and we all ended up on the pavement. The participants departed immediately afterwards, so they never did do the forms.

Summer holiday

It had been a difficult session with some angry people in the group. I gave a sigh of relief when it was over as I was catching a plane to Greece that evening. I cleared up, picked up my gear from the lobby next to the training room, and then discovered I'd been locked in. It seemed like the last straw. There was no phone, a thick oak door and high windows. I imagined the other holidaymakers getting on the plane. I shouted and banged on the door until a passer-by heard and went for the caretaker. 'How long could I have stayed here?' I asked. 'Oh, we're not using this room again until tomorrow,' he said. I picked up my things and ran.

14 Stage management

Anything can happen. The only thing you can predict is the unpredictability.

In this chapter, we consider the factors which participants, clients and even trainers often take for granted: time; the numbers of participants; the environment; support staff and their contribution; how people arrive on courses; and training props and other paraphernalia. All these factors play an enormous part in the smooth running of the training.

First, we consider time management from the points of view of the organization, the participants and you, before moving on to discuss how group numbers affect time and the group dynamic, and the importance of knowing the numbers to plan for.

The environment too has a bearing on the group dynamic, and we have some stories of ghastly places where trainers have been expected to work. We acknowledge that finding the perfect training room is not always possible, but we suggest some points to look out for. We then emphasize the importance of taking into account the support staff, the hidden group behind the training, and developing good working relationships with them. People who arrive with unrealistic expectations or are sent on an unsuitable course, and groups of mixed ability, are other perennial problems encountered by the trainer, and we determine some ways of dealing with these dilemmas. Finally, we explore the hazards of training props.

Untimely troubles

When you go to the theatre and you have paid good money for a seat, you expect perfect stage management. The performance must start promptly and if it's one minute late, you will probably glance at your watch. You expect it to start on time, with comfortable chairs, and warm or cool air conditioning, to be able to see and hear everything, and to know what you are there for. People coming for training have also paid good money – far more than the price of a theatre ticket – and therefore also have the right to expect first class stage management.

Time is money, and to value other people's time is to value them. Yet trainers meet innumerable problems relating to management of time. These untimely troubles can be caused by the *organization*, the *participants* or the *trainer*.

The tales that follow in each of these three categories were particularly untimely, and illustrate how organization, participants and trainer can all be the cause of time mismanagement. Ironically, but perhaps not surprisingly, several trainers told us that their most memorable time management problems had arisen when training 'time management'.

The organisation

- There is a culture of lateness.
- It is lax about time.
- They encourage people to go back to their desks at lunchtime.
- They put messages on the door for participants to follow up during their breaks.
- They are unrealistic about time and expect you to achieve a huge amount in a day.

Lockout

When I arrived the building looked deserted. The front door was open, but the door of the training room was firmly locked. I searched everywhere for someone with a key. I was doubly agitated. I had left early to be in good time, yet now I wouldn't have time to organize myself before the participants arrived. The time management trainer was about to set a memorable example.

Half an hour went by – still no key. There was no one in the admin office, so where were the handouts I'd asked them to copy? As if this wasn't enough, the first participants appeared. They queued and they waited. I felt it reflected badly on me, as if I were responsible for this havoc. I wanted to separate myself from it, without apportioning blame.

We eventually started time management – half an hour late. Most people, if annoyed, were polite about it, others were very angry, and determined to give me a hard time, thereby wasting even more of the day. I said I could understand their anger, but that it would be best to use the remains of the day to the full.

When the handouts arrived, they had been wrongly collated, so I reorganized them while the participants were doing group work, putting papers in piles inconveniently along the window sill. I wondered what they must be thinking.

While I flapped inside, I kept a calm exterior. Using my wit and my wits, and moving the activities at a slightly faster pace than usual, the group soon became absorbed and had a great day.

You have to laugh. What else can you do?

Where have all the people gone

I arrived an hour beforehand to be in good time, as I usually do. We were due to start at ten, but there was only one person there at the appointed hour. By half-past ten I was twiddling my thumbs and ready to go. Bored and tired with waiting, my adrenalin was gone. None of the participants seemed to see anything wrong in starting an hour and a half late.

Some organizations, and individuals develop a culture of lateness and are lax about time. They may not realize how their lateness affects others.

If you suspect that people will be lax about time, write to each person in advance, giving the itinerary and times and saying you want to start promptly. Ask them to contact you in advance if there is any difficulty.

The participants

- They are late.
- They are consistently late.
- They arrive far too early.
- They have no concept of time or timing.
- They don't respect your breaks.
- They keep looking at their watches – they're bored, or worse, find you are boring.
- They suddenly say they can't stay until the end.

Late . . . again

He was two hours late. He flung his coat on a chair, his crisps on the floor. He searched for his specs and folded his paper. 'Sorry I'm late', he said flippantly. The rest of the group glanced knowingly at each other and looked daggers at him, as if to say, 'Why does he always do this?' It wasn't the first time. He did it at every opportunity – morning, breaks, lunch. Pleasant and an excellent contributor to the group, he just couldn't get it together when it came to time. He was oblivious to the effect he had.

Bursting in

'Hello, sorry I'm late,' she yelled, bursting through the door and not sounding at all sorry. She was 40 minutes late and completely broke the flow of someone recounting a moving personal experience. The speaker was upset, the group stunned, I was furious. It struck me as selfish, attention-seeking behaviour. I could see the group visibly seethe, but no one spoke. I decided to encourage feelings to surface and then diffuse them. Otherwise they'd go underground and fester, waiting to erupt at some completely inappropriate moment.

Time is much more than the sum of the minutes lost. Issues to do with timing often spark disagreement: people lose their train of thought; the whole atmosphere of the meeting changes. How people value and respect each other is the fundamental issue at stake.

Where I have consistent problems with late arrivals and poor time-keeping, I interrupt the course and run an exercise with the group to explore their feelings about time. I ask everyone how they feel when someone keeps them waiting. 'How do you feel after five, fifteen, thirty minutes?' I ask them. 'Why do you feel like that?' I continue. 'Furious, irritated, I'm wasting my time, not respected,' they say. That way they answer their own questions about the significance of time.

GUIDELINES

To a great extent you can set the scene for people to observe good time-keeping when you begin the course by:

- Consistently being on time yourself.
- Starting on time, in the morning, after breaks and after lunch.
- Including time keeping in the group agreement. For example, no one can come in more than ten minutes after the start times except by prior agreement or for a very good reason, such as being delayed by a security alert. Also, people are asked to share the time fairly in plenary discussion and group/pair exercises. Then, when difficulties do arise, you can refer them to the agreement.
- Setting time structures for exercises and sticking to them, unless you specifically consult them about needing more or less time for a task.

- Explaining the significance of time: that is, it is more than the sum of the minutes lost.

The trainer

- You are late.
- You are late again.
- You are unclear to participants about times and timing.
- You misjudge the time you need for activities.
- You rush exercises.
- You don't fix times for breaks.
- You are inflexible about activity and break times.
- You let the training run into overtime.

Fireworks

I was driving through town, early evening, to do a time management session. I had left early, but not early enough. I'd forgotten it was Guy Fawkes night, and didn't know that I'd have to drive close to a fireworks display. After sitting powerless in the traffic jam, I finally arrived one hour late for the two-hour session. I blushed. They laughed.

I determined never again to drive to a training session without a mobile phone and contact number. I also try to keep abreast of local traffic and transport news.

No time to breathe

I made the mistake of arranging to see the Training Officer during my lunch break. By midday I was in need of a break and some space to myself. Instead, I had to be really on the ball. By the afternoon session I was worn out. I had not done myself or my participants any good by trying to make use of every minute.

I realized the adverse effects of lunchtime meetings. They are distracting, tiring and sap my energy for the task in hand.

During the break she kept asking me questions. I asked her more questions, trying to be helpful, to get her to sort things out. She was very needy, seeking my attention all the time. I felt that I had to make a special effort for her but in fact I just wanted her to go away. She didn't seem to appreciate that it was my break time too.

These days I ask people to respect my breaks, and to save their questions to ask during or after the session.

5,4,3,2,1

We had planned far more than we needed. We were fairly new to training and terribly worried we would not have enough material. So we rushed through most of it, constantly looking at our watches. More than once we told the group, 'Unfortunately, we don't have time to do that'.

I now realize the importance of taking things calmly. If you tell people that there isn't time to do something, they feel shortchanged. What you don't say, they'll never know, and taking constant decisions about what to include and what to omit from the course is part and parcel of good time management. Moreover, looking at your watch is definitely not on, it just makes people anxious, and they think you're not in control. Never finish up by saying, 'Had there been more time we'd have done x, y and z'. Your group will go away feeling that they've missed out.

I haven't finished yet

When I set group-work exercises, groups often finish at different times. It is particularly difficult when I ask them to come back into plenary and someone says, 'I haven't had my turn'.

Now I have handy additional discussion points for quick finishers, and I ensure that I tell people exactly how long they have in total for an exercise, and inform them at each stage when it's the turn of the next person in each group. I also like to walk round the room checking on how each group is doing during the exercise, but without being overly intrusive.

Time management tips for trainers

As a trainer you have to be a good time manager for yourself and for others, whether or not time management is one of the topics you train. Here are some time management tips for trainers:

- Notify the organization and/or participants of the dates, start and finishing times of the course.
- Provide a detailed programme, including duration, breaks, and if it's a sessional course, how much course work is to be undertaken in the participants' own time between the sessions.
- Include timekeeping in the group agreement at the start of the course.
- Include commitment in the contract, asking participants to attend the whole course.
- Include respecting your breaks in the agreement, so preventing unwanted intrusions and avoiding having to refuse people.

- Prepare detailed time plans for the course, the constituent activities, and for each part of each activity.
- Allocate more time when you have a large group, especially for the plenary parts of exercises.
- Be flexible, allowing extra time for matters of real interest to the group.
- Be adaptable, shortening or omitting exercises as you judge appropriate. Making snap decisions while you're training can be aided by indicating in different colour highlighters in your activity plans which elements are (a) essential (b) medium and (c) least important.
- Give an appearance of being calm and unhurried, however aware you are of how much you have to do.
- Leave enough time for debriefing each activity and evaluating the course.
- Make sure that you and your participants have clear-cut breaks. You may want to give more frequent breaks to those who are unused to training or to doing sedentary work.
- Give yourself proper breaks, away from the group, and give the group time away from you.
- Finish the course at the time you have stated. It is better to be a little early than to overrun, unless you agreed the extra time with the group, or it is at their request.

Count me in: Numbers

The numbers in a group affect timing, content and the dynamic, and knowing how many people are attending obviously means that you can plan accordingly. But however organized you are, if you work in a variety of places, you will have experienced situations like those below.

> We sat there – the four of us – waiting for the others, until we realized that there would be no-one else. I was expecting twelve, but illness, drop-outs and very little publicity had taken their toll. All my ideas for small group activities had to change.

> 'Could you run a session for us – there will be about twenty.' He wasn't entirely clear. There were forty-five and me.

As you become more experienced, you learn to adapt the course to different numbers, but how the participants will benefit from the training will be very different.

Small groups

Small groups can get to know each other and you well, but problems arise if there is a difficult or dominant person in the group, or participants' interests do not coincide.

The concentration required from all of you is immense but also rewarding. But make sure that you allow natural breaks as well as those planned.

GUIDELINES

- Be careful not to dominate or lead all the time. Give the group opportunities to talk without you. This can be difficult and it could look as if you were opting out, but it allows the group time to consider matters without always looking to you.
- Offer individual exercises and spend time with each participant.
- Even in a small group, split it up occasionally so that they work in pairs. Then you bring the ideas together.
- Let participants adapt the agenda to their own requirements, but also keep them within the established framework. If you find yourself with a much smaller number than you had expected, make sure that you keep to the programme which they received beforehand, but give more time for them to follow up their particular interests.

Large groups

Large groups need much more organizing and much of the training time is taken up by this. You have to be more directive.

GUIDELINES

- Allow time for working in smaller groups, and also make sure that these change. Don't always leave it to them to choose who they work with. Think up ways of mixing the group such as giving people a number, and suggesting working with people you don't know, or with people who do similar or different jobs. Plan all this beforehand if you know that you will be working with a large group.
- Make sure you give all instructions clearly. Someone is bound not to hear.
- Allow time for movement and check that each group is clear what they have to do.
- Spend time with each group at some stage in the day. If possible, create an opportunity for you and those individuals who don't speak up in the group to talk to each other directly.

- Make sure that the dominant voices in the large group are not the only views that are heard by using the small groups to discuss issues which might be controversial.
- Use the feedback time efficiently so that it doesn't become repetitive. Rather than just repeating back what people have discussed in a group, ask a follow-on question which uses their conclusions but moves the discussion on.
- Sum up clearly and have handouts for people, containing the main points.
- When you read the evaluations, remember that it's very hard to please everyone in a large group.

Your place or mine: The training environment

If you train in a regular place, you can adapt it to your requirements, regularly check equipment and make it training-friendly. Most trainers, however, have to adapt to all sorts of conditions. A group of them together will regale you for hours on the places they have been. Like the one holed up in her hotel room the night before the training – the only woman pursued by a congress of American boxers. Or the trainer who had to work hard to overcome an enormous distraction:

I remember when we had mice. You never knew if they were going to run across the floor or drop off the ceiling beams.

Training organizers are not always aware of how much the environment affects the learning, and how the venue, not you, gives participants head-aches or sends them off to sleep. The acoustics, comfort, heating and decoration all help or distract from the training. Dealing with a room full of nauseous participants because of the kitchen smells is asking a lot from any trainer. Working in a room with partitions puts paid to any idea of confidentiality:

I felt all the time that other people could overhear. It was like working in an open-plan office. There was another group training at the end of the room, so I was worried about disturbing them. Now and again I'd ask people if they would please keep their voices down to an acceptable level; at other times, we needed the freedom to laugh and talk loudly. I found the whole experience very uncomfortable.

Even when you think you have found a good place, the atmosphere can be wrong:

> I was pleased to be training in what sounded like a very pleasant hotel. But it turned out that they had converted two bedrooms into the training room. The ceiling was too low, the decoration heavy, and somehow, the atmosphere felt inappropriate – even without the beds.

Most trainers don't expect perfect or luxurious conditions, but you do need to take into account how much the environment has added to the final effect of the training. Researching the venue and, where possible, seeing it before you start, will help you enormously in planning. You can arrange the room so that the participants are not distracted by, for example, jazzy curtains. Find out if it is suitable for the kind of training you are doing. Can people move? Is the furniture adaptable? Are the rooms for small group discussions nearby and comfortable? Whatever the conditions, make sure people have opportunities to move round. Encourage them to take some fresh air during the breaks, and you do the same.

If you are experienced in looking for good venues, you'll probably agree that what helps trainers and participants alike are:

- plain carpets;
- comfortable chairs, but not the kind you want to sleep in;
- non-fluorescent lights;
- natural light;
- easily moveable furniture;
- rooms where the heat is consistent, so that you don't have one participant complaining about the cold, another about the heat;
- comfortable heating;
- tables that are large enough for people to put their papers on;
- flipcharts, attached to the wall at a reasonable height for writing on;
- space to move around;
- a space where everyone can see each other; and
- a place for coffee and tea which doesn't involve a long walk or going to another building.

Support staff

Support staff are usually invisible, often taken for granted, yet they work hard behind the scenes, and are essential to the smooth running of the training. Occasionally, they are show stoppers:

She was talking about a very important issue at work. Everyone was interested and concentrating. There was a loud knock, no wait for the answer; a woman drove the trolley across the floor noisily and then proceeded to rattle the cups and saucers.

Seeking out the support staff and discussing arrangements with them beforehand can stop this kind of occurrence.

Catering staff have a difficult time when trainers run over time or suddenly demand different menus. Administrative staff too need clear instructions from you, lists of what you want, and time to photocopy or collate materials. If you are working with technical staff, you will want them to be at their very best for your work. It is you who will field the criticism when things go wrong, but you receive the plaudits when everything works without a hitch. You need good management skills and a creative approach when there are difficulties to overcome. Blaming the support staff doesn't work; thinking through the problem and involving them in solving it does. If the stagehand forgets a crucial prop, improvise – the show must go on.

GUIDELINES

- Explain the aims and objectives of the training to support staff and how they can contribute to its success.
- Acknowledge the importance of their job and give them time to do it.
- Explain what you want clearly avoiding technical jargon.
- Emphasize and support them when participants complain unjustifiably or treat them badly.
- Create a good working relationship with the support staff, thanking them and informing their manager of their contribution to the training.
- Develop a partnership with them so that they are clear about their own role and yours. Future training arrangements together will then work well.

Horses for courses

Unrealistic expectations

What sort of course is this?

'I'd have liked more videos.' As I read this young person's evaluation, I thought, yes, and I bet he'd have liked pizza with it too.

People who see training as a day out, or as a time to sit back and receive 'the knowledge', receive a nasty shock when you ask them to think the issues through, come up with their own ideas, or actively participate in an exercise. Sometimes this is because they have never experienced training like this before; they have attended training which is purely skills-based or which offers one clear-cut formula for working. Or they are looking for the short cuts, quick tips.

We are not saying that offering skills is not part of the trainer's role; it certainly is. But if you are making the learning personal to participants, they need opportunities to try it out and analyse what they are doing. Videos, for instance, are useful for illustrating points or inspiring people by example, but they don't take into account participants' differing learning needs.

GUIDELINES

- If groups are unused to active training, explain why you work in this way and how they are likely to benefit from it. At the end, talk about what they have learnt. If participants are still critical, talk about what the advantages and disadvantages of this style of training are.
- Don't criticize other types of training that people have attended simply because their approach is different from yours.
- Recognize that participants may need a lot of prompts and clearly set out exercises if they are not used to contributing to the training.
- Look out for those who are seeking short cuts or quick fixes, and involve them actively in the work. Give helpful hints, when appropriate.
- If you are using videos, stop and discuss at short intervals.

The wrong course

There are those who are sent or find themselves on the wrong course.

I could not understand why they were on the course. It only had general relevance to their job as they described it. 'Why have you chosen this course,' I asked. 'We didn't,' they answered, 'but our department is committed to Investors in People and is sending us on everything.' Although the five of them remained on the course and were very amenable, it did affect the content because their interests were different from the others. I followed it up afterwards and realized how important the procedures for attending courses are.

Hey you, get off my course

'Do you think this course is right for me?' she asked. 'No.' I thought, but said 'Yes' and immediately regretted it. I knew she would try to hijack the course. It was neither what she wanted nor needed. She already had the skills I was offering and her needs were at a deeper level. It would be better if she didn't attend, but because I found it hard to say 'No,' I had placed myself in a difficult situation, and would have to find some escape route. There were two possibilities, neither very comfortable: to go back to her and say 'I've been giving it some thought and I don't think this course will in fact meet your needs'; or to let her start the course but suggest she leave if my concerns were realized.

GUIDELINES

- The more precise the pre-course information is, the more likely the right people will attend.
- Check who is coming and what their roles are. Before the training day, find out yourself or through the training organizer as many details as possible about why the participants want to attend and whether they have discussed this with their manager. Ask what they want to achieve from the course. This may be done through a questionnaire. If you think the course is not suitable, discuss this with them, or, if necessary, their manager.
- If people for whom the course is only partly relevant want to stay, keep to the main objectives of the course. Involve them, but don't allow them to dominate or take the content off track.
- Suggest people leave the course if it's not relevant to them.

Mixed abilities

I prepared the course assuming that I was going to be with one particular type of worker. When I arrived I found that the group were completely mixed. Not only were they working in different ways, but also they had very different experiences and abilities.

This situation, the trainer found later, is not uncommon, and so she no longer treats it as a problem.

You can expect to meet people with different levels of learning and ability in any group. Part of your skill is to:

- plan programmes where you can treat people as individuals;

- enable people to recognize the knowledge they have and how they can best use their previous experience; and
- encourage the group to use their differences positively and work with them.

They will, after all, have to work with people whose skills and experience differ, but will also complement each other.

The technical hitch

Trainers who work abroad have many tales to tell of the 'harsh' environments they sometimes work in and are therefore prepared for anything:

> You name it – there's no room, no participants, no equipment.

But even working in your own country, few of us complete our training careers without coming across some technical hitches. You are certainly not the only one for whom the flipchart always seems to fall apart:

> I have frequently been in full flow and all my flips descend onto the floor.

These hitches call for resourcefulness and a certain aplomb on your part, but they can so easily put you off your stride:

> This happened years ago but I can recall it as clearly as if it happened yesterday.
>   The group I addressed was so large I had to use a lapel microphone. I was so nervous I hardly ate the night before and only picked at my breakfast. By late morning my stomach thought my throat had been cut and protested loudly. I was so far back from the group I felt confident that no one could hear the rumble but I had forgotten about the sensitivity of the mike. Hearing your tummy rumble over the loud speakers in front of a room full of people doesn't do much for one's ego.

Other trainers will tell you of wrongly collated handouts, or handouts that are not ready or have gone astray in the post; it is all part of the rich experience of training. It's panic stations at the time, but the story is often told with a laugh in retrospect. Then there's equipment that doesn't work properly, like the slide projector which would only take two slides at a time and kept jamming, thus failing to enhance your image as the well-prepared trainer. Having to fix flips onto boards or rails put up by someone about 7 feet tall who has not stopped to consider that even in high heels, you will never reach, does nothing whatsoever for your dignity. The overhead bulb going once is manageable, but when it fuses for the third time, then you wonder why you ever spent all those hours creating your magnificent transparencies.

The video monitor with poor reception may infuriate the personal development trainer and, like some trainers, you may avoid technology as much as possible. But when technology is a key part of the training and plays up, then the trainer needs highly creative solutions:

> You arrive not knowing who has set the systems up, or their skill in doing so. The equipment is unfamiliar. I've learned not to trust the technology so when it turns against me, I'm prepared to train technology without using technology – as far as I can.
>
> I was training abroad on an intensive 5 day course with demanding training targets. I needed every moment. I arrived to find the machines still in boxes and the software not loaded up. The delegates had paid mega money and had mega expectations. Luckily, my lack of trust in technology and consequent 'just in case' preparation paid off.
>
> I used to full effect the three days it took the support staff to set up the technology, by: giving participants detailed background of what they could do and how; employing other media, such as handouts and overheads; and leading group discussions on the theory. Once the technology was ready, I used the remaining two days to the absolute maximum for practical, hands-on training.

The increasing use of technology has improved presentation and helps enormously, but fortunately it hasn't entirely taken over from the personal touch. You still control the content of the presentation, and if that is properly prepared, you can always carry on in most circumstances.

With all the available high-tech at your disposal, it's possible to print glossy booklets on personal computers. The emphasis on good marketing means that the outside presentation can become more important than the content. Certainly, beautiful handouts may help people, as this trainer explains:

> I use different bright colours with bordered paper, and people become quite excited, asking, 'What's coming next?' I find it helps them to remember what is on the handout; they remember the colour or the pattern.

She also emphasizes that this is not achieved at the expense of the content. The handouts may be beautiful, but they do need to relate to real work; they are a back-up to what you are doing or a further item for participants to work on. Organizations with very small training budgets may not be able to afford the latest equipment, but they can still produce relevant and useful materials.

Summary

- Work on the assumption that if equipment can go wrong, it will. Therefore, always make some 'just in case' preparation. Relying entirely on a video, for instance, is asking for trouble. Have an exercise ready which you can use while you obtain another recorder or mend the existing one.
- Give yourself time before the course to check the equipment in the room. Participants don't want to see you fiddling around with the video as you try to find the fast forward button or focus the projector.
- If you work with support staff, talk to them about what you want, when you will be using the equipment, and how you will work together.
- Do any photocopying, or preparation on your computer, with time in hand. The chance of the photocopier breaking down is much higher when you do it at the last minute.
- Always have back-up materials. You can always photocopy your own set of handouts if the participants' copies haven't arrived, even if, as one trainer comments, 'It cost a fortune on the hotel copier'.
- Overhead screens and projectors are notorious for malfunctioning. Use them if they really do help, but if people can't see them, it is better if they have a personal handout to read from.
- Present clear slides and transparencies. Too much on them is distracting. Just copying from a textbook and putting that on the screen means that the print is often unclear and much of it won't be relevant.
- Find out how to use technology to your advantage, to give you more time rather than more aggravation. High-tech is developing fast, and many organizations are well equipped with the latest technology. You can use software programmes to produce overheads and slides, and some organizations have equipment which allows you to plug your computer straight in to project them. With computers in every school, you are dealing with an increasingly computer-literate audience.
- The more you know about how to use the equipment the better. You are then not relying solely on support staff or a helpful participant. Participants will often help you, but remember they want to proceed with the course, not watch you panicking.
- Always check beforehand what sort of equipment there is, and plan

your programme accordingly. You don't want to find that your video cassette isn't compatible with the apparatus when you arrive.

- If you are videoing participants, make sure the equipment is set up beforehand.
- When things go wrong with the technology, don't take it personally. Be prepared to change the way you train.
- See yourself, not the equipment, as the greatest resource. You are!

15 The Oscars

They say goodbye and suddenly you see what they really think.

We begin this chapter by describing what evaluation is, and determining why and when we evaluate, showing in the process how evaluation takes place verbally throughout the course and how to deal with any disparaging comments. Then we examine the evaluation sheets, giving some examples of the questions that you might want to ask, and recognizing that they vary according to the course and context. We go on to suggest ways of making them more interesting to write for those who have completed many, and easier for those who find them difficult to write. We discuss what you do if you have to assess participants on a course and how you give general feedback. We study the reactions trainers experience when participants pass their judgements on the training, and how to interpret their comments. Finally, we analyse the impact of endings on everyone.

The whole relationship changes as you give out the evaluation forms: the participants suddenly have power, whereas you had the power before. You don't fully discover how they use that power until you sit and read the evaluations after they have gone.

There is no other job that we know of where you are evaluated every time you do it and by people who don't know how to do your job. If you work in an office you may be appraised annually or six-monthly. People may check over what you do, but you don't strive for or expect an Oscar a day, though you're pleased when someone says, 'Well done'. So why do you crave an Oscar for every performance? Why do you need to ask 'Did they think I was great?'

Evaluation

What is evaluation?

Evaluation concerns the value of a course to the participants, the organization and you. One organization sees evaluation on four levels: reaction; knowledge and skills; application and business results. The *reactions* come from participants towards the activities, environment and learning experience. The participants and trainer assess the *knowledge* and *skills* gained. Participants *apply* skills during the session to workplace situations, and develop plans of action to take back to work. The organization is able to assess the *results* for the effectiveness or profitability of the business.

Why evaluate?

> I ask myself time and time again about evaluations, what is the point of them? Does anyone ever read them?'

Participants evaluate, you evaluate, the organization evaluates. From the combined evaluations you decide what to retain, what to change and what new training is needed.

The trainer is probably the one person who will definitely read the evaluations. On occasion, you design them for your own use. At other times, the organization drafts them without consultation with you. When this happens you are not always sure whether they are to assess the quality of the trainer, the course content, staff development or to identify further training needs.

Participants give you their immediate response to the course, at the end, but you don't necessarily have any way of knowing how people translate their new skills to the workplace. Long term evaluation is helpful in discovering the impact of the training and how to develop any further courses. The in-house trainer is in a very good position to do this, but as an external trainer you might wish to follow up too. You could, like one organization, carry out a follow-up six months after the event, writing to every participant if you have the administrative resources to do so. Talking to the Human Resources Manager or Director of Training gives you a means of evaluating your own performance and how relevant the training has been.

When do you evaluate?

Evaluating takes place before, during and after the course, and enables you to make changes at any stage. You are most likely to receive verbal feedback during the course and written feedback at the end.

Pre-course

Useful pre-course feedback can help you effect changes to the existing course even before you begin, and can put you on track for next time.

> I had written to every participant asking them to bring to the course a 'to do' list of 20 pending tasks, I had given my phone number in case of queries. Sure enough, there was one. 'Is this a personal or work "to do" list?' they asked. Next time I wrote the letter I was able to correct it and pre-empt questions of this nature.

In the beginning

In addition to the written evaluations at the end, there are the spoken comments made during the course. However, even as participants introduce themselves they may tell you what they think of the course. They may be reluctant attenders and so prejudge you and the course. Or perhaps they had no choice but to turn up:

> 'I'm here because of my appraisal which was pretty useless anyway,' he explained. I said, 'I sympathize with you being sent on a course. Actually it's also hard for me, knowing that people don't want to be here.' Immediately, we understood each other. We were allies.

In the middle

There is much time and opportunity for participants to give you hostile feedback of a verbal nature during the course itself. Examples of this type of feedback cited by trainers include: 'This is crap!' 'You don't know what you're talking about.' 'This is just namby-pamby rubbish.'

While these may take your breath away at the time, you at least have the opportunity to challenge, seek clarification from their originator, and work towards a more constructive relationship. How do you manage such personal jibes? One trainer describes her approach as follows:

> I show the person that I have in fact really heard them and am taking their comments seriously. I say their words, however rude or crude, back to them: 'Why do you say I'm crap?' 'Why do you think that I don't know what I'm talking about?' 'I'm interested to know why you describe it as namby-pamby rubbish. Can you explain that to me?' I try to address them calmly and with no hint of judgement in my voice, however I may feel personally.
>
> One thing's for sure – they get quite a surprise when they hear their

own words and expletives repeated back to them by me. They can't avoid answering when you're so direct, and when they've been unpleasant, but you remain pleasant. It helps them to think about what they've said, and why they are saying it.

The important point is to create an opportunity for genuine dialogue. Of course you can't force anyone to discuss matters with you, but you can try. After that, I can move them on to thinking about what they will gain and what they can give to the course.

Personal derogatory remarks are not everyday occurrences, but they are biting when they come. For the most part, participants are positive and constructive with their feedback. By giving them regular opportunities to feedback, such as at the end of every activity, you will have the chance and the knowledge to build on good ideas and to rectify those that don't work on both current and future courses.

At the end

At the end of the course comes the written evaluation, viewed by many participants as a boring piece of bureaucracy.

If you haven't been involved previously in drafting the evaluation form, it's not always relevant to your training. However, as the trainer, there are some points you will want to know. Ideally, you want the form to:

- separate your role as trainer from the content of the course;
- ascertain if the content was relevant for the participants;
- find out if the exercises worked; and
- check what else they would have liked included and their further training needs.

It would also be interesting to know if they enjoyed themselves, and to have some reassurance about yourself and the course.

Some trainers like the forms to be anonymous. However, this does mean that you can't identify who said what, or follow up useful or controversial comments or matters of concern.

I train people to take responsibility for their feelings and actions, and when they are actually invited to renege on this by evaluating anonymously, I am very annoyed. It gives some people the green light to vent their anger on the trainer, but more problematic is being unable to contact the person who feels bad and help them find a way forward. I feel helpless.

The evaluation sheets

Evaluation sheets range from very simple to highly sophisticated. What is appropriate will depend on who you are working with and whether or not they are used to completing them. It is helpful to remind people at the top of the form of the course objectives. That is, 'The course objectives were: . . ., . . ., . . .' Here are some examples of questions that trainers have found useful:

- How well do you think the course objectives were met?
- What did you like most about the course, and why?
- What did you like least about the course, and why?
- Did you enjoy the training? (On a scale from 'Very much' to 'Not at all')
- What aspects of the training were most interesting or useful to you personally and why?
- Were any aspects of the training difficult to manage? If so, what were they?
- Was there anything missing from the course that you had expected?
- Is there anything you would have liked more time on, and, if so, what?
- Was anything given too much time?
- How well were equal opportunities and anti-discriminatory practice integrated into the training?
- What have you gained from attending this course?
- How will you use this training in your work?
- Who will support you in putting this into practice?
- Please comment on the trainer.
- How did the group help you in your learning?
- What did you think about the information provided before the course?
- How did you find the training environment? (Room, chairs, heating, air, lighting, equipment, refreshments, etc.)
- What suggestions do you have for improvements overall?
- Any further appreciations?
- What other training would you like to attend?

Introducing the evaluation sheets

You need to set aside time – already in limited supply on a short course – for participants to do the written evaluations. Trainers complain about losing precious time on evaluation sheets while others find themselves apologizing for them to their group.

Some participants want to rush through the form in two minutes flat, which is unlikely to do justice to your hours of preparation and all the energy and thought you have expended during the training. They often ask: 'Can I do it later and send it back to you?', but you know that if you agree to this you are unlikely to see it again. Allocate enough time to evaluate creatively. Trying to do it in two minutes at the end is unfair to you and to them, and doesn't work anyway.

Making it interesting

Dealing with the boredom of evaluations can be a challenge, especially with regular course goers who find them tedious. You can almost see their hearts sink as you say, 'I'd like you to fill out an evaluation.' This can be because:

- If they have attended other training they will have filled out many such forms before, and are therefore bored by it.
- They are genuinely tired at the end of the day.
- They want to get back to their office, or have a bus or train to catch.
- They find the form complicated, or dislike any kind of form filling.
- They simply can't think of what to say.

Some trainers simply give out the form and collect it in again without comment. However, participants need guidance as to the purpose of the form and how to be specific in their feedback if you want them to produce something you can usefully use.

When people are new to training and hence unused to writing evaluations, it makes it easier if you turn it into a stimulating activity. Sitting alone filling out a form requires a level of mental energy from your participants which they may not have by the end of the session. If you create methods to obtain evaluations of your training which are more enjoyable than filling out a tax return, it's more fun for everyone, no matter how seasoned they are.

First, remind them of the course objectives as written in the course description: Secondly, refer back to their original expectations of the course, and review those you have covered, and those which were omitted and why. They may want to follow up some of these in the workplace or through further training.

Togetherness

Trainers describe their different approaches to obtaining evaluations. Here are some examples:

- You can ask them to work in threes: to discuss the course and how they felt about it; to determine in what ways they have developed as a result of it; and to consider what they liked and what else they would have wanted.
- Invite them to write group evaluations, combining their similar and dissimilar comments or completing the forms individually. This is particularly helpful for those who are new to training or lack confidence in their written skills.

Brick wall

Another activity is to ask everyone to think of three topics or learning points that have been important to them on the course. Hand each person three slips of paper, designed to look like bricks, and ask them to write one on each 'brick'. Then they blu-tak their bricks to the wall, building a wall of importance and learning.

Post it

People enjoy finding out what others have thought about the course, so this method and the brick wall increase their interest in the evaluation. Ask them to answer questions and write their answers on Post-it notes, which they stick on the wall for everyone to see.

Brainstorm

If you opt for the more traditional approach to evaluation – that is, you give each person a form to write individually in silence – you can still make it easier and lighter if you first brainstorm in plenary on to a flipchart one or more of the following:

- What did you like about the course?
- What didn't you like?
- What would you have liked to be different?
- What have you learned?
- What changes will you make as a result of the training?

Multiple choice

Some organizations have evaluations in the form of multiple-choice questions. Participants can choose to circle a selection of comments from 'A brilliant day' to 'A complete waste of time'. This is easy for them to do, though not exactly subtle, nor are they required to substantiate their views.

In summary

There are many differing ways of conducting evaluations, but try to observe the following:

- Allow sufficient time.
- Do evaluations well before the end
- Turn them into an interesting activity which stimulates and helps participants recall.
- Make it as easy and as much fun as possible.
- Vary your method of evaluating according to who your participants are.

Evaluating your participants

You may have to evaluate your participants during the course. These evaluations may be formal assessments for accredited training. Thus both you and the participants need to be clear concerning your precise role in this exercise, and they need to know what you are assessing. You can only assess how they perform in the session. It is not your responsibility to assess how they put their learning into practice afterwards.

You can comment on observable and demonstrable skills like the ability to write a report, use a spreadsheet, listen to others or summarize. If managers ask you to assess their staff, make sure that you all know what is expected. Keep your integrity and the trust of your participants, making it clear that you can only assess what you see and what takes place in the session. Everyone needs to be clear about how and to whom you will be giving your assessment after the session, and it is preferable if the participants see what you say.

You act as a role model for feedback, and in courses such as presentations skills, assertiveness, and interviewing skills, you may be asking other participants to join in this too. Spend time talking about how you give positive helpful feedback. Give participants examples of demonstrable competences and show them how to give clear evidence to back up what they say. For example, if the participant could not hear the speaker, make sure, first, that they say why he or she personally thinks this, and second, that they own the feedback by speaking in the first person. Show them how difficult it is to take feedback when it is not specific or you are given too much.

Participants want feedback that helps them learn. As one said:

> I don't want someone just to say 'Well done' when I don't actually feel
> that pleased by what I've done. I want to feel that they've really looked

at or listened to what I've done, and, if it's good, to tell me why, and if it isn't, to give me some ideas of how to change it.

All alone

> And when they've all gone home, you sit there all alone, in an empty room, sometimes elated, sometimes deflated, but alone.

You can be left with a great sense of isolation as the once buzzing room empties, leaving you alone with their frank comments about you and your work. You may feel worn out, but you still start to read what they say.

How do you feel?

> I agonized for days over why a participant would want to be so hurtful.
> I've more important things to do than worry about one day's lousy training.

What people write, and say, can affect you deeply, and sometimes it is meant that way. If you are feeling particularly fragile, emotionally or physically, the feedback may feel worse than it is.

It helps to put things in perspective if you think back on how you have felt when you have been participating and evaluating. As one trainer describes:

> As I give out the forms I wonder what they think about me and I'm reminded how I have felt as a trainer when I've participated on someone else's course and evaluated their training. I've ranged from envious to jealous, relaxed to competitive, disdainful to admiring, and that affects how I fill out my form. At other times, it's a straightforward matter of chemistry – I liked the trainer or I didn't.

What they say

We are concerned here with negative and difficult feedback, how you respond and how you feel about comments such as:

- 'The trainer was too nice.'
- 'The trainer was too young.'
- 'The trainer didn't know enough about the organization.'

- 'The trainer was unprofessional.'
- 'The trainer ignored the objectives.'
- 'It was too rushed.'
- 'It was too easy.'
- 'I didn't understand a thing.'
- 'The course was too short.'
- 'I hadn't expected it to be so demanding.'
- 'I felt worse at the end than I had before I began.'

Though comments like 'This is best course I've ever done' cheer you, the jibes of unhappy participants can be hard to manage, especially if you feel they are unfair and you know that you have invested hours preparing for their benefit. You may allow the barbs to overshadow the appreciative words of those who have learned and valued your training. So how do you make sense of it all?

Negative comments take many forms. They may appear in the written evaluation as specific and helpful:

> 'I would have liked more time on how to delegate an unpopular task to my staff.'

or unspecific and unhelpful:

> 'This has been a total waste of time.'

The first example is helpful because the participant is making a clear suggestion as to how you could improve the course. You will also have to take into consideration the views of others on the course: would they have wanted more time on this topic or not? It is that overview that will help you decide whether to adjust the time allocation on your course next time. You may also have dealt with this at the outset by checking who wanted what from the course – that is, their needs and expectations – and so will have made the adjustment at that point.

However, as in the second example, comments such as 'total waste of time' feel personal, and are often meant to be taken that way. Try *not* to take it personally, as the comment itself may say more about the person who made it than about you and your training.

The trainer as interpreter

As trainers, we all have to take great care in how we interpret negative evaluations. At times you leave with a great sense of satisfaction and even elation; other groups bring you down.

Where to make changes

It can be hard to forget the barbed comments of the angrier and more dissatisfied customers – they come back to haunt you, especially when things aren't going so well. You have to take great care not to overreact, and to balance the negative with the positive feedback you receive. You must separate the genuine criticism from the sarcasm and jibes, so that you can respond appropriately. You either use the comments as a means to improve and make changes, or you listen then discard, recognizing that you have achieved what you set out to do, and what you and your participants agreed upon.

You can ask yourself these questions:

- Was this person angry at being sent on the course?
- Did someone misidentify their training needs?
- Were they feeling depressed about themselves/the organization, and hence could see no point in doing anything?
- Were they on the wrong course – hence it was a waste of time for them?
- Were they alienated by something that happened during the training?
- Can you picture anything that you could have done to help them feel more positive about their training experience?

In addition, if you can identify who the unhappy participant is and you have a means of contacting them, – for example, when you are in-house – you could ask them:

- Why did you say in your evaluation that the course had been 'a complete waste of time'?
- What would you have liked from the course?
- What would have left you feeling that it had been a worthwhile experience?
- What could I have done to enable you to benefit more?
- What could you have done so that you could have benefited more?

You could also suggest that when they attend training in the future they take more responsibility for their learning by speaking up during the course instead of complaining afterwards. However, they may come up with this answer themselves in response to the last question above.

When do you act on what they say?

So who is the judge in all this? Is it you, or is it them? And what do you do as a result? What do you take seriously? In effect, a balance has to be struck: you assess their comments in the light of what you know about the individual, what happened in the group and what is going on in the organisation. You need also to take account of whether there is a generally held view in a particular group, or a recurring view about your training, or whether it is the isolated remark of one individual.

Here are examples of when to act or not on some of the comments listed previously:

- *'The trainer was too nice'.* They probably wanted to feel more challenged by you, wanted more constructive criticism.
- *'The course was too packed and rushed.'* Slow down your pacing next time. Check with the group from time to time, as different groups need different pacing.
- *'It was too easy.'* You can't act on this unless you are able to check in what way they found it too easy. Balance this comment against how the rest of the group found it: was it satisfactory for them?
- *'The course was too short.'* Try to agree an extension to the training. If they want a longer course, they must have felt a benefit. A comment like this is often a mark of success.
- *'I felt worse at the end of the course than when I began.'* A comment like this at the end of a personal growth/confidence/stress management type training can be cause for concern. Find out why and what they feel they need. Point them in the right direction for having those needs met by providing relevant information/contacts. This kind of comment is another reason why names on forms are so important; you will want to follow up a comment like this, but if the forms are anonymous you won't know, unless it's obvious, who wrote it.

A good sense of self-esteem is a helpful asset for any trainer: prickly comments and strong negative reactions from participants can truly test how you value the quality of your training, and your approach and style in the delivery. It is a self-respecting and respectful trainer who is able to assimilate points as he or she sees fit, and then to analyse, incorporate and amend. As one trainer describes:

> They're telling me how to improve and showing me how to avoid problems in the future, so I consider any comment carefully. I also share it with my main contact and explain (a) how I think it arose and (b) what I'm doing about it.

I find the evaluations very useful. They help me in my own self-development. They show me the parts I don't see. They make me aware of the huge range of experiences of different people on the same course, I can take all these factors into account and then decide 'I must remember to do that next time'.

In discussing how to handle negative comments, trainers offered the following invaluable advice:

- Use specific questions in an effort to elicit specific answers.
- Try not to justify your actions, approach or the material.
- 'Listen' well – to the spoken or written words.
- Put yourself in the other person's shoes.
- 'Listen' to the feelings behind what the person is saying
- Consider how their behaviour in the course relates to the evaluation.
- Try to separate what is your responsibility and what is the other person's emotional baggage
- Attempt to keep the negative feedback in proportion.
- Ask for concrete examples of what they did not find helpful and what would have been helpful.
- Obtain substantive clarification of non-specific comments.
- If you consider that their views are valid, make appropriate changes.
- If you think they have not substantiated their viewpoints, recognize that you don't deserve it and discard the criticism.
- Try not to allow negative feedback to grow out of proportion and rankle with you.

You can also forestall some of the negative feedback, and the unhelpful ways participants convey it, by:

- Having sight of the organization's evaluation form before you prepare your course
- Clarifying at the beginning to the organization and the participants the extent and limitations of what you will cover and what they can expect to gain.
- Notifying people in advance of the course objectives and who the training is aimed at, so that they can be selective and choose if your course is suitable or not for them.
- Using questions on the evaluation form that elicit specific examples from participants and encourage them to make practical suggestions about how you could improve your training.
- Asking participants to write their name on the evaluation sheet, as they

are more likely to take a responsible approach to completing it when they do not have the protection of anonymity.

● Asking them verbally to give specific examples of what they liked or what they would change, as you take their views seriously and their feedback will help you retain the positive aspects as well as make improvements. In the words of one trainer, 'If you are not satisfied, please don't tell me it's rubbish, as I can't improve on that. Tell me what was rubbish, then I can act accordingly.'

● Giving participants sufficient time to complete the evaluations – in fairness to yourself. Remember, you have given much time, thought and energy to your participants, and now it's their turn to give time and thought to what they have received from you.

Evaluating back to the organization

Talk to the Human Resources person or manager who initiated the training about how the course went from your own point of view. Make sure that you don't breach any confidentiality agreement you took, or reveal individual identities or personal information intended for the group's ears alone.

Ideally, the organization will have a structure for you to feedback your own written comments in the form of a trainer's evaluation of a training session. Points to be addressed could include:

● how it went from your point of view;
● un/successful aspects;
● aspects to be reviewed or altered;
● the environment, catering and equipment
● course administration; and
● the three-way communication between the administrative staff, yourself and participants.

In reporting back, you might consider whether the objectives set and content offered were appropriate, and also realistic within the time scale; whether the objectives of the organization coincided with the needs of the participants; and what other needs were identified. Were there any requests that the group wanted you specifically to take back to the organization?

It is also an immense help when someone comes in and talks to you at the end, debriefs with you, goes through the evaluations with you, and takes a genuine interest in the training. You need some support for yourself as well as an opportunity to say how you saw it.

Talking to your peers

You sometimes ask yourself, 'Was it them or was it me?' It's easy to blame yourself when the training doesn't go well. Thus evaluating it with other colleagues is enormously helpful, since it may be more to do with the group than with you.

> It took me several hours to reach my destination for a very short session. I came away wondering what I had actually achieved? What was the point? They didn't seem interested, and yet I had tried so hard. I rang up another trainer and told him my experience. 'It's not you,' he reassured me. 'I had exactly the same experience.'

All our goodbyes

We have talked so far in this chapter about the trainer's feelings at the end of the day; here we stop to think about the participants. You spend time on beginnings with your group, but endings too have a powerful impact on everyone.

You work hard to make a positive ending, and then someone turns round and says: 'It's all very interesting and I've enjoyed it, but I can't see it working in our place.' There is a mixed message here that you have to respond to quickly, pinpointing something that he or she could do in order to go away feeling proactive. Participants' negative feelings at the end are not unusual and can occur despite their satisfaction with the course.

There will be participants who will be pleased that the training is over, who can't wait to leave. But some will feel dejected by leaving a person or group they had become close to. Others will feel they are losing support and are going back to handling matters alone again. The danger is that such feelings may affect adversely the closing moments of the course, and you have to avoid that happening.

> We came back after the break, everyone laughing, positive and ready for the final session of the two days. Then she started – telling us how awful her work was, how she hated it – it was difficult to stop her outburst and I could feel myself and the group becoming depressed and all our optimism and energy draining away. She hadn't said all this during the course, but had been quite positive about what she did. I knew that if I allowed her to go on, we would all go out feeling dejected. I had to stop her. She could not be allowed to have the last word, yet obviously she needed to express these feelings.

Where you can, talk with the person afterwards, but keep the group in mind. Endings may trigger all sorts of feelings, so allow ample time to debrief the last activity and the course as a whole, and stay around so that you can talk to individuals afterwards. Let each person express their end of course feelings, goals and intentions. Set up a structured but flexible, way of doing this. At the very end:

- Thank the participants warmly for their input, and, if appropriate, express your enjoyment at working with them.
- Suggest they exchange telephone numbers if they want to keep in touch with each other.
- Ask them to find a mentor if you have been training a subject like time management, someone who will encourage them to apply the skills and techniques from the course back at work.
- Allow five minutes before the end for them to arrange a reunion. The wish for this may arise if the group has been together over a long period, or has shared a profound experience, or has simply had a great time together. You can send a list of names round, but don't organize it for them.
- Say that you will speak to the director if they want a follow-up course, while making a mental note that follow-ups may seem a good idea at the time, but don't always happen. People and events involved move on, sometimes as a direct result of your training.
- Be absolutely clear about the ending: 'I'm closing the formal proceedings now' and/or 'Please leave your evaluations on the desk and you are free to go when you're ready'.
- Notice the person who looks, during or at the end of the session, as if they need something more. Personal development training in particular can trigger emotions which have been dormant, and you have a responsibility to direct that person to an appropriate source of help, which may or may not be provided by you.

Trusting in yourself

If you trust in what you do, try not to allow yourself to feel unduly hurt and upset by brickbats that you receive. Recognize that these are par for the course, something you are bound to receive at some time by virtue of the fact that you train people, then ask them their opinion of the training. There will always be those who are angry with themselves or with others and will vent their emotions on you. There will be those who don't know how to feed back constructively or who refuse to do so. Some people quite simply won't like you; as one trainer says: 'They are entitled not to like me', and though this may be hard to accept, 'you cannot win 'em all'.

Having a sense of when you train effectively and when you don't, being able to deal with personal comments in a professional manner and to respond appropriately to negative feedback, is all part of the skill of being a trainer.

Epilogue: The magic of training

It's the magic in someone's face as the penny drops and the light goes on. They suddenly realize they can do it.

Training is tough. But the rewards can be immense. This book has covered troubleshooting in training. We close by recording what trainers have said to us about the magic, which lies in seeing your input make a difference, whether it's in helping people develop hard skills, or in enabling them to go back to work and resolve a difficult situation. Your rewards are both personal and professional, such as hearing about the difference you have made to an organization as well as to individuals, especially when this comes from someone with authority.

Trainers constantly talk of the challenges:

> It's the challenge of having to be so different each time, sometimes gently nudging the process forward, at other times using every skill personally and professionally to move things along.
>
> It's enormously challenging, using everything you have, every jot of experience, skill and ingenuity to work with the dynamic and chemistry.
>
> I find it's a constant reminder personally and professionally that I don't know everything. The moment you become complacent is when you can lose it.

Moreover, trainers can have a profound impact for the better on someone's life and can derive huge pleasure from that:

> One conversation can be so important; it may be the only chance you have.

> We can do so much in so short a time. I've learned never to under-estimate the impact of even a few words. A short time spent with people can be highly therapeutic and last for the rest of their lives.

They hear about the impact face to face or in writing:

- 'A vital, entertaining performance by an exceptional motivating trainer.'
- 'I felt inspired to take all the information back to the office. It filled me with confidence.'
- 'This has changed my life.'
- 'The day was a breath of fresh air, blowing away the cobwebs.'
- 'I come back to your courses because you give me a great boost.'
- 'I can't wait to get back to work tomorrow. I really want to deal with this.'

Then there are the pleasant surprises:

> Their body language says, 'I know everything', but by the coffee break they're saying to me, 'You're someone who could help me'.

> I watched a nervous, inhibited participant deliver a polished presentation. She came back next session and said 'I've done it'.

Trainers spoke of their enjoyment in meeting each new group and working with many different cultures, and they say that they 'get a great buzz' from a range of experiences:

- Feeling skilled and competent.
- Being up there at the front.
- Being the centre of attention and being able to show off.
- Dealing with the challenges of people disagreeing, being reluctant or hostile, and turning this around.
- Having their own thinking challenged.
- Having to think on their feet.
- Enabling a group to come together and work creatively.
- Watching people resolve a problem in front of their eyes.
- Knowing that people are fired with enthusiasm at the end of the session.
- Seeing them go away with positive action plans and the determination to put them into practice.

Later they hear about individuals using the skills or techniques well beyond the course:

I'm thrilled when I see people move forward positively, or feel that the training has given them insights, and confidence to use those insights.

I see the energy and inspiration they've derived.

People contact me months later to tell me how they've changed their life.

It's amazing knowing you can have a profound effect on someone's life.

I feel part of someone's 'enlightenment'.

Trainers have described how they do need to like training to go on with it. They may experience days that are hard, and with scant reward, but they have to have an overriding faith in people. There is so much to be learned from groups. As one trainer put it:

It's a privilege to work with people at a particular point in their lives.

So when a participant comes up to you and says, 'You really have made a difference to me. I could never have done it without you,' accept the compliment, but gently remind them, as this trainer did:

I can't take all of the credit. You've done so much yourself.

Sources and resources

This appendix contains details of sources which we have found useful or have been recommended by other trainers. There are innumerable products on the market and this list makes no claim to be exhaustive. However, the items included here offer a rich variety of information and resources for training. Most of the materials referred to are available by mail order.

Reference

Dictionary of HRD by Angus Reynolds, Sally Sambrook and Jim Stewart (Gower)
Provides succinct definitions of more than 3000 terms, together with explanations of acronyms and abbreviations and a list of journals of interest to HRD practitioners.

Handbook of Management Games and Simulations, 6th edition, by Chris Elgood (Gower)
Part 2 of the *Handbook* comprises a directory of some 300 games and simulations, with detailed information about each product, appropriate indexing and a list of relevant publishers/distributors.

Interactive Directory of Learning Resources (Gower/Open Mind)
A PC-based directory containing details of over 4500 learning resources from more than 90 publishers and indexed by subject, topic, keyword, medium and publisher.

The Training Directory (IPD/Kogan Page)
A comprehensive listing of consultants, training providers, training materials and product suppliers.

Publishers and producers

BBC for Business
Books, videos and multimedia

Woodlands
80 Wood Lane
London W12 0TT
Tel: 0181–576 2361
Fax: 0181–576 2867

Daedal Training Limited
Packages, games and activities, mostly print-based

309 High Street
Orpington
Kent BR6 0NN
Tel: 01689 873637
Fax: 01689 874183

Fenman Limited
Videos and print-based resources

Clive House
The Business Park
Ely
Cambridgeshire CB7 4EH
Tel: 01353 665533
Fax: 01353 663644

Gee Publishing Limited
Looseleaf subscription services covering all aspects of human resource management, with regular updating. Publishes the monthly *Personnel Manager's News*, produces management videos and, in association with IRPC Group Ltd, offers courses.

100 Avenue Road
London NW3 3PG
Tel: 0171–393 7400
Fax: 0171–393 7463

Gower Publishing Limited
Books, activity manuals and videos

Gower House
Croft Road
Aldershot
Hampshire GU11 3HR
Tel: 01252 331551
Fax: 01252 344405

Peter Honey Publications
Workbooks, activities and manuals, including material on learning styles

Ardingly House
10 Linden Avenue
Maidenhead
Berkshire SL6 6HB
Tel: 01628 33946
Fax: 01628 33262

IPD Books
Books and print-based resources

IPD House
35 Camp Road
Wimbledon
London SW19 4UX
Tel: 0181–263 3387
Fax: 0181–263 3333

The Industrial Society
Books, videos and print-based resources

Robert Hyde House
48 Bryanston Square
London W1H 7LN
Tel: 0171–262 2401
Fax: 0171–706 1096

Jumpcut
Video resources, especially on training young people to prepare for work

Bank Chambers
2 Lidget Hill
Pudsey
West Yorkshire LS28 7DP
Tel: 0113 256 6544
Fax: 0113 236 0056

Kogan Page Limited
Business and training books, series and packages

120 Pentonville Road
London N1 9JN
Tel: 0171–278 0433
Fax: 0171–837 6348

Lifeskills International Limited
Books, workbooks and activities

Wharfebank House
Ilkley Road
Otley
West Yorkshire LS21 3JP
Tel: 01943 851144
Fax: 01943 851140

Management Learning Resources
Distributors of a range of books, disks, videos and activities

PO Box 28
Carmarthen
Dyfed SA3 1DT
Tel: 01267 281661
Fax: 01267 281315

Maxim Training Systems Limited
Training and self-development materials on disk and CD-ROM

61/63 Ship Street
Brighton
East Sussex BN1 1AE
Tel: 01273 204198
Fax: 01273 738829

McGraw-Hill Book Company
Books and series for the professional trainer

Shoppenhangers Road
Maidenhead
Berkshire SL6 2QL
Tel: 01628 623432
Fax: 01628 770224

Melrose Learning Resources
Leading producers of training videos

Dumbarton House
68 Oxford Street
London W1N 0LH
Tel: 0171–637 7288
Fax: 0171–580 8103

National Extension College
Resources and manuals covering vocational and general education, teaching, counselling and community health

18 Brooklands Avenue
Cambridge CB2 2HN
Tel: 01223 316644
Fax: 01223 313586

Open University Press
Books covering group process, group membership, intergroup relations, the impact of race and culture on relationships, and counselling and therapy

Celtic Court
22 Ballmoor
Buckingham MK18 1XW
Tel: 01280 823388
Fax: 01280 823233

Pfeiffer
Books and videos on management and HRD, mostly US in origin

Campus 400
Maylands Avenue
Hemel Hempstead
Hertfordshire HP2 7EZ
Tel: 01442 881891
Fax: 01442 882288

Pitman Publishing Limited
Books and series for training professionals

128 Long Acre
London WC2E 9AN
Tel: 0171–379 7383
Fax: 0171–240 801

Training Direct
Videos and computer-based materials

Longman House
Burnt Mill
Harlow
Essex CM20 2JE
Tel: 01279 623927
Fax: 01279 623795

Video Arts Limited
Leading producers of training videos

Dumbarton House
68 Oxford Street
London W1N 0LH
Tel: 0171–637 7288
Fax: 0171–580 8103

Journals

Many membership organizations produce their own magazines or journals. The British Association for Counselling, for example, publishes *Counselling* which, as well as featuring articles relevant to counselling, reviews training books and manuals and contains information on accredited training courses.

The following are published by:

MCB University Press Ltd
60–62 Toller Lane
Bradford
West Yorkshire BD8 9BY
Tel: 01274 785200
Fax: 01274 777700

Career Development International
Empowerment in Organisations
Industrial and Commercial Training
Journal of European Industrial Training
Journal of Management Development
Training and Management Development Methods
Training Network
Training Tomorrow

Other magazines of interest to trainers include:

Organisations and People
Association for Management Education and Development
14–15 Belgrave Square
London SW1X 8PS
Tel: 0171–235 3505
Fax: 0171–235 3565

People Management
Personnel Publications Ltd
17 Britton Street
London EC1M 9NQ
Tel: 0171–336 7637
Fax: 0171–336 7646

Training Officer
Fenman Training
Clive House
The Business Park
Ely
Cambridgeshire CB7 4EH
Tel: 01353 665533
Fax: 01353 663644

Training Technology and Human Resources
MR Publishing Limited
International Centre
Spindle Way
Crawley
West Sussex RH10 1TG
Tel: 01293 531105
Fax: 01293 537003

Professional organizations

Association for Management Education and Development
Brings together management development specialists from consultancy, formal education and the organizational world both private and public. Offers a variety of learning activities (many of them regionally based) and interest groups.

14–15 Belgrave Square
London SW1X 8PS
Tel: 0171–235 3505
Fax: 0171–235 3565

The Industrial Society
Focuses on the people element of business success, offering an extensive programme of training courses and conferences. Membership benefits include telephone advice, use of library, quarterly journal and monthly newsletter.

Robert Hyde House
48 Bryanston Square
London W1H 7LN
Tel: 0171–262 2401
Fax: 0171–706 1096

Institute of Management
Provides a range of materials and services designed to help managers to improve their performance. Accredits management courses leading to qualification at Certificate and Diploma levels.

Management House
Cottingham Road
Corby
Northants NN17 1TT
Tel: 01536 204222
Fax: 01536 201651

Institute of Personnel and Development
Promotes public understanding of training and develops recognized standards. Offers and accredits courses for personnel and training professionals leading to NVQ and diploma qualifications.

IPD House
35 Camp Road
Wimbledon
London SW19 4UX
Tel: 0181–971 9000
Fax: 0181–263 3333

Resource centres

Stockists of training materials in all formats from a range of publishers/producers. Most will offer advice and viewing facilities in addition to sales and hire.

Boldu Limited
The Learning Centre
3 Farm Street
Hockley
BIRMINGHAM B19 2TZ
Tel: 0121–523 3199
Fax: 0121–523 7010

Cambridge Training &
Development Limited
Block D2, The Westbrook Centre
Milton Road
CAMBRIDGE CB4 1YG
Tel: 01223 582555
Fax: 01223 582551

Cristo Human Resource
Development
The Old Mill
New Tythe Street
Long Eaton
NOTTINGHAM NG10 2DL
Tel: 01159 727160
Fax: 01159 462147

The Equitas Group
The Grange
Hayford Lane
STOWE HILL
Northants NN7 4SF
Tel: 01327 349130
Fax: 01327 349242

Flex Training
9–15 Hitchin Street
BALDOCK SG7 6AL
Tel: 01462 896000
Fax: 01462 892417

GW Resources
5 Winckley Court
Winckley Square
PRESTON PR1 8BU
Tel: 01772 202721
Fax: 01772 202722

Hallamtechnic Limited
South Point
South Accommodation Road
LEEDS LS10 1PP
Tel: 0113 246 8321
Fax: 0113 246 9798

Hallamtechnic Video
Waverley House
Effingham Road
SHEFFIELD
S Yorks S4 7YR
Tel: 01142 754546
Fax: 01142 751918

Intelligent Training Solutions
29 Narrow Street
LONDON E14 8DP
Tel: 0171–791 3000
Fax: 0171–791 3030

International Organisational
Leadership
26 Sandyford Office Park
Sandyford
Dublin 18
IRISH REPUBLIC
Tel: 00 353 1 295 4766
Fax: 00 353 1 295 7820

International Organisational
Leadership
Ashwell Farm
Dolton
WINKLEIGH
Devon EX19 8RF
Tel: 01805 603495
Fax: 01805 603495

The Learning Combination Ltd
West England Management Centre
The Promenade
Clifton Down
BRISTOL BS8 3NB
Tel: 01179 257373
Fax: 01179 737447

The Learning Combination Limited
Smiths House
45–49 High Street
CORSHAM
Wilts SN13 0EZ
Tel: 01249 701048
Fax: 01249 701049

Learning Resources International
Limited
Bamfords Yard
Turvey
BEDFORD MK43 8DS
Tel: 01234 888877
Fax: 01234 888878

Learning Resources International
Limited
Business Development Centre
Duncan House
High Street
Stratford
LONDON E15 2JB
Tel: 0181–215 0706
Fax: 0181–215 0709

MRA International
The Clock House
18 Grove Street
WANTAGE OX12 7AA
Tel: 01235 770 067
Fax: 01235 771 167

North East Training Services
Abbey House
Hadrian Road
WALLSEND
Tyne & Wear NE28 6HH
Tel: 0191 295 0076
Fax: 0191 263 3161

Open Mind
Delphi House
Deanfield Avenue
HENLEY-ON-THAMES RG9 1UE
Tel: 01491 411061
Fax: 01491 411531

Progressive Training
Canada House
Fiend End Road
Eastcote
RUISLIP
Middx HA4 9NA
Tel: 0181–866 4400
Fax: 0181–429 4121

SCET Scottish Council for
Educational Technology
74 Victoria Crescent Road
GLASGOW G12 9JN
Tel: 0141–337 5000
Fax: 0141–337 5050

THE Business & Human Resource
Centre
Castle Works
East Moors Road
CARDIFF CF1 6XQ
Tel: 01222 332072
Fax: 01222 332154

TMS Insight
The Cedars
39–41 Compton Road West
WOLVERHAMPTON WV3 9DW
Tel: 01902 20999
Fax: 01902 20666

Training Associates
Hanborough House
Hanborough Business Park
Long Hanborough
OXFORD OX8 8LH
Tel: 01993 883790
Fax: 01993 883408

Training Helpline
57 Malvern Road
HORNCHURCH
Essex RM11 1BG
Tel: 01708 738888
Fax: 01708 738888

Wessex Transport Training
4 Victoria Road
FERNDOWN
Dorset BH22 9HZ
Tel: 01202 875373
Fax: 01202 875982

Office supplies

Office World
Supplies equipment ranging from flipchart pens and OHP material to computers and software and office furniture. For direct mail catalogue telephone 0800 424444.

Viking Direct
Offers a wide range of stationery, furniture and equipment, available from retail outlets throughout the UK and by direct mail. For catalogue telephone 0800 500024.

Using the Internet

Trainers are making increasing use of the Internet. It provides instant access to information on training consultants, journals, providers, publishers and resources including interactive multimedia software. You can also create a website to promote your own services.

Useful books for Internet beginners include:

Sandra Vogel, *First Steps on the Internet*, Aurelian Publications, 1997
Angus J Kennedy, *The Internet and Worldwide Web: the Rough Guide*, Rough Guides Ltd, 1997

Index

accredited training 152, 188
activities in training 39–40, 72, 107,
    111–2, 115–9, 165, 168, 169
administrative tasks 74–5
    see also support staff
agreements between trainers and
    trainees 106
    see also group contracts
anecdotes in training 30, 107, 125, 151
anger 9, 64, 91, 95, 104, 105, 118, 123,
    128, 131–2, 133, 140, 146, 147, 164,
    191, 196, 200
anonymity in evaluations 184, 193–4
anxieties
    in trainees 94, 106, 116, 117, 118, 147
    in trainers 43, 55–67
appearance of trainers 97–8, 153
appraisals *see* evaluations of training
arguments 16
assertiveness 24, 62, 157, 160
assumptions 33, 38, 154
atmosphere for training 24, 25, 26, 172
    see also environmental factors in
        training
attacks on trainers 121–2, 133–4, 146,
    183–4, 196
authority 6, 24, 27, 59, 62, 98, 99, 152
    see also power
awareness 110

back-to-back training 74, 79
balance in training 147–56

beginning sessions in training 97–102,
    166–8
behaviour 38, 64, 85, 86, 97–102, 103,
    107–8, 109–10, 115, 121, 123–4, 126,
    127, 138–9, 140, 141, 145, 148, 152,
    193
belligerence in trainees 103
    see also anger
bereavement (effect on a trainer) 59–61
body language 16, 100, 104, 126, 127,
    138, 142, 147, 200
    see also eye contact
boredom 16, 25, 37, 44, 72–3, 127
    in evaluations 186
brainstorming 134
    in evaluations 187
breaks 29, 32, 71, 93, 108–9, 111, 114, 165,
    167, 168, 169
burn-out 78

case studies (use in training) 116
caucuses 100, 151–2
challenge 27, 121–2, 130, 131, 132–3, 146,
    199, 200
change 9, 16, 26, 33, 81, 130, 146, 191,
    193
    management of 86–9
charisma 7, 30
co-training 27–32
commitment 32, 53, 168
communication 12, 49, 85, 140, 157
competence 29, 200
    see also skills